Christmas

Dear Mark.

Hope that you have enough information in this book. Love,

Grandma + Grandpa.

THE MAKING OF A PILOT

THE MAKING
OF
A PILOT

by
Ed Richter

The Westminster Press
PHILADELPHIA

PHOTO CREDITS

Photos in Part I: Courtesy of Cessna Aircraft Co.

Photos in Part II: Courtesy of Trans World Airlines

Photos in Part III: Pages 101 and 145 by the author; all others courtesy of U.S. Naval Photographic Center

PUBLISHED BY THE WESTMINSTER PRESS ®
PHILADELPHIA, PENNSYLVANIA

PRINTED IN THE UNITED STATES OF AMERICA

INTRODUCTION

This is not a "how to fly" book, although it's probably a distant cousin; the nonflying reader should be able to learn how pilots drive aircraft. But the primary purpose of the book is a little different.

Imagine, if you will, a person who's curious about flying—maybe even considers it as a career. Without too much trouble today, he can get reams of information about aviation. If he's a high school student, his guidance counselor can painlessly point him in the direction of a good college, and even suggest helpful courses. The military services will be happy to help. (They need pilots badly, and the need continues to grow.) Even the airlines, with ever-expanding needs, will cooperate by offering these hard facts of where to go, what to study, and what to expect when he's finished.

But the one thing he finds it almost impossible to get is the *feel of flying*. What does it feel like to drive a 600-m.p.h. jet around the sky, at maybe 35,000 feet, with a hundred and more passengers sitting back there staking their lives on your ability to do your job? And how do those pilots learn their trade, anyhow?

What's it really like to fly a jet fighter onto a pitching aircraft carrier, at speeds of well over 100 m.p.h.?

How does it feel to solo an airplane for the first time?

What are the sights, the sounds, and the smells of flying? What do commercial pilots talk about on long, seemingly boring trips? Are some pilots really afraid to fly?

The purpose of the book, then, is to answer those questions—to re-create for the reader the aura of flying airplanes.

To do this, I spent about a year on research. The result is a three-part book (private, commercial, and military flying). In Part I, the purpose was to introduce the reader to flying. I tried to recall exactly how I felt as a student pilot; how I progressed through the earliest stages of flying lessons; and the thrill at being permitted to solo an airplane. I remembered my instructors by name, and I inserted their names into the narrative because it seemed natural and warm and human to do it that way. That's the way it really happened. And I included my mistakes as well, because that's the way they happened too.

For the research on Part II, I spent much time with people from one of the world's biggest airlines, TWA. I visited their training school at Kansas City, flew coast to coast in jet cockpits, and talked at length with many pilots, instructors, administrators, and ground personnel.

I chose Naval aviation for Part III because I believe that the aircraft carrier pilot represents the epitome in flying skill, combined with the most obvious hazards. Any man who can land a whizzing jet on a rolling deck, and hit a tiny cable with a tail hook, is a pilot indeed. Sometimes they do it at night.

I visited the U.S.S. *Forrestal* at sea to get the information for that part of the book. I talked with everyone from an admiral to a deck crewman—and especially with pilots. I heard their complaints, watched them train, listened to their fears, and flew with them.

In the course of doing the research, I accumulated many editorial debts. I owe much gratitude to many people—far too many to mention in this short a space. But a few stand out:

First, I would have been almost helpless without the tremendous assistance of a great gal, TWA's Amy Kelley of that airline's Philadelphia office. She arranged for so many

6

things, so well, that a stranger might have thought I was a vice president of the airline.

Similar thanks have to go to Lt. Cmdr. Dan Dagle of the Navy, headquartered in Washington. The man's a real genius at making arrangements for little things like riding aboard an attack carrier, and lunching with admirals.

I also want to thank the Cessna Aircraft Company, which provided me with the latest photos and technical data on a whole line of general-aviation airplanes.

Bob Kadoch, the veteran TWA pilot whose story is featured in Part II, spent so much time with me that I began to feel like a jet jockey myself. And his good friends Chuck Hasler, Bob Magrey, Charlie Church, and Rudy Couk (the latter is chief pilot of Pacific Airlines) were generous in their assistance.

I'm also grateful to TWA's Bob Helmer, who guided me through the company's Kansas City complex, and to Captain John F. Rhodes, who checked my manuscript for technical accuracy.

And, finally, I owe thanks as well to the crewmen of the U.S.S. *Forrestal*; to the flying Navy at Willow Grove (Pa.) Naval Air Station; to Keith Justice and all the fine people working for TWA at Philadelphia International Airport; to TWA's San Francisco personnel; to the Navy's *All Hands* magazine, for my Chapter 14; and to hundreds of others, including a fine manuscript checker, Jane Bradshaw.

PART
I

CHAPTER 1

"It's not the long fall that gets me; it's the sudden stop."

"Flying is hours of sheer boredom punctuated by moments of stark terror."

"If God had wanted me to fly, he'd have given me wings."

I've heard them all, and dozens like them, since I took up flying in the mid-1950's. I've even come up with a few replies of my own: "I don't want to be the best pilot in the world, I just want to be the oldest." And "If God had wanted me to drive, he'd have given me four wheels and a carburetor."

For several years, I carried around in my wallet a yellowed clipping that documented a good (but negative) argument in favor of flying. It said, in neat statistical tones, that more people were killed on tractors last year than in airplanes. (I finally threw it away when one of my friends said that it proved he shouldn't be driving tractors either.)

All the clichéd arguments prove one thing to me: in the minds of a lot of people, flying remains a weird and extremely hazardous means of transportation today.

Maybe it's because air deaths always appear so dramatic. After all, there's not much of the exotic left in auto deaths anymore. We can kill 35,000 people in a single year on highways, and it doesn't make the headlines that one plane crash does—much less a toppled airliner with sixty or a hundred people on board.

But against those ghastly accounts is the realization that thousands of flights are made every day in which the most serious incident is the pilot's failure to remember where he left that half a cheese sandwich. Some fourteen hundred flights are made out of Chicago daily. That goes on day after day, month after month, year in and year out, without headlines.

One crash, and every newspaper's city room grows frantic; millions of readers shudder.

In reality, air crashes are not only rare—they are probably investigated more thoroughly than any other form of accident. The Government spends hundreds of thousands of taxpayers' dollars digging into commercial crashes in order to answer one question: "Why?" And Uncle Sam doesn't waste any time in doing something about them, either. Hundreds of times each year, he proclaims in do-it-or-else tones that "modifications" must be made on certain airplane parts. And thousands of owners, from the big airlines to the weekend pilots, must comply or have their aircraft grounded.

Training, too, is more solid. To get an automobile license in my state you take a quick physical and a simple written test. Then you prove to a trooper that you can safely navigate that feather-light power-transmission monster at 10 m.p.h. through a parking place, and onto a little bit of a fake roadbed. Do it and you're cleared for turnpike traffic.

Did you ever see one of those newly licensed drivers in heavy traffic? He makes me nervous to watch him. We give him 300 horsepower, turn him loose on people, and wonder why, when he mauls a six-year-old on a bike.

It doesn't happen that way in aviation. If anything, I was a better pilot when I first got my license than I am now. I was flying regularly then, two and three times a week. Now when I get the time to fly, I have to practice by myself for a while before I dare take passengers. (Little Junior, meanwhile, having been duly licensed to steer that Drive-Mor

Super 8, eagerly takes Grandma for a spin around the block. Not *my* grandmother, thank you.)

The basic training course to receive a private pilot's license is crammed into a solid forty hours of actual flying time, plus a good deal of homework on the ground. In addition, there is a rugged two-part written examination, and an exacting physical.

(Once issued, the private pilot's license is good forever unless revoked. But the physical must be repeated every two years in order for the license to remain valid.)

I'll guarantee you this much: that newly licensed private pilot *knows* how to fly his airplane safely. If he doesn't do it —well, that's another matter.

And, unfortunately, enough private pilots *don't* fly safely. There is always the pilot who wants to take off in marginal weather, or fly through something beyond his qualifications. Basically the limits of one's skills are drilled into the fledgling pilot—hard. Weather formations are part of the course. So are dire warnings about how quickly your license can be suspended or revoked for infractions of the federal rules.

I had one such close call a year after I received my own license. I flew into Newburgh, New York, after having duly notified the Federal Aviation Agency of my intentions by filing a flight plan. The routine flight plan is not mandatory for this kind of flying, but it can save your life. You tell the FAA (in person or by radio) where you're going, by what route, and also what kind of equipment you have available. They automatically get word of your progress as you check in with other stations en route, and they check you off when you close out the flight plan at the end of your trip. If they haven't heard from you, they start looking. The proper procedure is to radio in at your destination and tell them you've arrived. Or you can do it in person after you land.

In this case, however, we were a little late and overly anxious to drive away with the people who were meeting us at Newburgh. I forgot completely about the flight plan. Later that afternoon, during a leisurely lunch, our host asked me about flying. "Do you have to check in with anybody when you make a trip like this?" he said. It was a casual enough question, but . . .

"Ugh! I forgot about the flight plan! Where's the phone?"

I quickly called the local FAA office, and went through the embarrassing and painstaking procedure of checking in two hours late.

What I got in return was the worst dressing down I'd received since I'd been in the service. I was lucky to avoid a fine or suspension.

The lesson is simple: Don't foul up, because the whole machinery of Uncle Sam is behind you. It's there to help, and you'd better learn to use it the right way.

Come to think of it, that sums up the whole of flying. The machinery is there; it's up to you to learn how to use it. The same lesson holds true whether you're flying a single-engine Cessna or a four-engine jet carrying 150 people. Everything is there, tested. It's your job to make it work the way it was intended. That means, in short, that you have to work at it.

Making it work can be tricky. There are unfamiliar controls, strange instruments, and interestingly different procedures. Everything is organized in the sky and along the airways; it has to be, or there would soon be chaos. There aren't any traffic lights or yellow lines painted along your path, but there are signals strangely like left-turn lanes, and roadway markers. And violating them is as serious at 5,000 feet as it is on the ground.

There are other rules too. One of the first is to know your aircraft. Here again, the difference between driving and flying can be startling. A driver—licensed by his state and experienced in one auto—can legally buy a new car and drive it anywhere, at any legal speed, without being questioned. But that kind of action would be foolhardy in a strange airplane.

Airplanes react differently, and there can be quite a difference between flying an 85-horsepower two-seater and a 150-horsepower four-place model. So while you can change from a Corvair to a Cadillac with relative ease, you'd better not try it in flying. Not unless you've grown tired of living.

Changes in autos are ridiculously simple, but highly underrated. I drive a Volkswagen, and I like to think that I have mastered the machine. But when I recently rented a Dodge with power controls, and found myself on an expressway after five minutes' driving time in the new car, I felt inadequate to the task. The speed limit was 65, but I moseyed along at a safe 50 until I got the feel of the shiny new car at my fingertips. Even then, I had an unusual amount of difficulty getting adjusted when I got into heavy traffic. And when I reached the congested city streets, with six-way intersections, I was the slowest driver in Chicago. (Three days later, when I returned the car after having been in the driver's seat for perhaps eight hours, I felt confident and secure in handling it.)

Yet I wonder how many people make that kind of change with unseeming fear—planning a long trip, for instance, on the day they take delivery of the new car. No experience whatever in the new model, and away they go . . .

It's not only foolhardy, it's also illegal in airplanes. The Government's licensing agency demands a lengthy get-acquainted session, plus some solid flying experience, especially in takeoffs and landings, before you're checked out in a new aircraft. I have been flying for a number of years, but a qualified instructor told me recently that it would take at least twenty more hours of flight time to qualify in a fast new plane basically similar to the one I'm used to piloting.

It's all based on rather sound principle.

Airplane crashes don't merely happen. They are caused. Something, or somebody, *makes* them occur. And one of the easiest ways I know to get hurt in an airplane is to try flying one without the proper background. "He's just an accident looking for a place to happen" is a slogan I've respected for years. As I have said smilingly before, I don't want to be the best pilot in the sky, only the oldest one.

The man who taught me to fly stressed, time and again, that safety is hard work and that "accidents" are not actually accidents. Eugene Trigiani, a veteran pilot and a good one, had never had anything approaching an accident in all the years before he began working with me. And in the years since, his flying record has remained unblemished. He doesn't believe this is the result of luck, either. He is one of the most fastidious men I know. It takes him quite a while to prepare for a flight, and he does everything according to the book. This may get annoying after a while, and inspire impatience, but it has kept him very much alive in the midst of a business that can kill quickly if you let it. And his training has kept me alive too.

Back when he was teaching me the ropes, Gene was full of slogans and humor-laden advice. He had me working like a machine myself—almost automatically. The airplane machine and the man machine, working together in order to fly.

My response to different flying situations was drilled into me, again and again, until I performed them automatically. I remember wondering whether it was all necessary, whether he was overdoing it, whether it was that painstaking. But he didn't let up, and I kept responding.

A simple maneuver like a turn, which comes in the first or second flight lesson, was drilled into me: "Look left, left rudder, left aileron," he'd say. And I can still hear him, whenever I make a turn. I don't think I've made one left turn since, in an airplane or a car, without first *looking* left. The point is that looking *has* to precede turning. You can imagine how idiotic it would be to turn *without* looking. But you also know that a lot of people do it. Watch the

*A pilot makes S-turns across a road
as a practice maneuver.*

next driver you accompany. A quick glance in the rearview mirror and he's "ready" to change lanes on a turnpike. Some pilots do it that way too. They merely assume that there's plenty of room in the sky for them, and they flit across into a sharp turn without ever having looked.

Some of them aren't flying anymore.

Another procedure of Gene's stuck with me so hard that I had to laugh about it one day. From straight and level flight, the procedure to descend was to pull out the carburetor heat lever, wait thirty seconds, then ease back on the throttle.

During my training period, I was flying solo one day near a major airport. Straight ahead of me, some ten miles away, was a big airliner. We looked to be at the same altitude, and I decided that I had better move my little two-seater down. All I had to do was to push the control stick forward slightly. Instead, I reacted automatically. I pulled out the

17

carburetor heat, waited for the longest thirty seconds of my short flying career, and descended. I must have lost maybe 1,000 feet of altitude before it dawned on me what I had done. By that time all I could do was to laugh aloud at my machinelike response to a situation.

Gene Trigiani didn't laugh when I told him about it. He said it proved that I was learning how to fly properly, by making myself do things without thinking about them.

I made other silly mistakes. Shortly after my first solo flight, I was alone in the Aeronca, flying within a few miles of Gene's Bethlehem-Easton (Pennsylvania) Airport. It was an hour short of dusk, and I decided to land.

I approached the airport correctly, following the traffic pattern that every pilot knows by heart. But when I was ready to make my last turn, toward the runway, another pilot cut me off. He turned inside my turn, and headed down. He landed a few moments later, while I was still on my final approach. His turn had shaken me; I had assumed that he would have gone behind me, following me in my long approach to the field. I felt he had violated a rule, and I wanted to tell him so.

When I landed I sought him out. But instead of my telling him, it was the other way around. "Look, son," he said, with a tone dripping pity for my ignorance, "there are other guys up there too. You made a turn that left you two miles away from the runway. Three planes could have landed in the time it took you to get down. What were you doing out there?"

I was playing it safe, I thought. I was making wide turns, to be sure. But I had seen in them added safety. In actuality, they were time-wasting turns. And they were inconveniencing other pilots trying to follow that same traffic pattern. He had grown tired of waiting, and had made the proper turn himself.

On another occasion, my shortsightedness cost Mohawk Airlines a few dollars, and gave two of Mohawk's pilots a near-fit. I was landing at Glens Falls, New York, up in the Hudson valley, and it was my first experience on a long hard-surfaced runway. I decided to test my own skill by trying to put the plane down within the first twenty feet of its 5,000-foot length.

I made it, in a perfect three-point landing. What I didn't think of was that I now had something like a quarter mile ahead of me before I could taxi *off* the runway. And one of the prime rules of landing is to clear the active runway as quickly as possible.

My little putt-putt taxied slowly, and I drawled along for what must have been a half minute before it began to dawn on me that I was cluttering up the main runway. I decided to look back. In order to do that in this airplane, you have to fishtail it—make a sharp left and then a sharp right on the ground, looking back out of the side windows (there is no rear window).

I turned and saw what looked like the biggest Convair ever made, booming in on me at what appeared to be the speed of light. Fortunately for me, the pilot had enough sense to go around again. And by that time, I had found the nearest taxiway, and had parked my plane.

I got out, scampered up to the terminal, and sat behind a newspaper, trying to look as unpilotlike as possible while the Convair pulled in to the gate. Its two pilots got out and walked over near my plane, muttering something about those crazy private pilots who thought every airport was built for them.

I mumbled a prayer of thanks for their schedule, which forced them to take off a few minutes later.

In reality, that didn't qualify as a close call. There was no imminent danger, despite the sensation that I was about to be flown into. The pilots were waiting until the last minute before committing themselves to another costly go-around, in the hope that I would be off the active runway by then. When they saw that I couldn't make it, they merely went around. But it was a foolish mistake, nevertheless, and it taught me indelibly to get off runways.

In a sense, all of flying is like that. Each mistake teaches you something, and you aren't supposed to make the same mistake twice. The purpose of training is to provide you with an opportunity to make errors while under the proper supervision. After you're licensed, you are supposed to have passed the stage of making the worst ones.

You'll still make some dandies, though. I know a private pilot who landed at an airport twenty miles from his destination, and didn't know it until he parked his airplane. And another friend of mine once landed a seaplane downwind (it's always *into* the wind that you land and take off) despite the fact that dozens of pilots around him were landing properly. He thought *they* were wrong!

The making of a pilot is work plus common sense plus more work. And, to be honest about it, a lot of fun.

"What constitutes a good landing?" I once asked an instructor.

"Any landing you can walk away from," he grinned. But that same instructor was inside the airport office one day when I landed rather bouncingly on the main runway, a quarter mile from where he was standing. When I walked in a few minutes later he greeted me with: "Hi, Ed. I *heard* you land. I figured it was you."

CHAPTER 2

The *making* of a pilot. It's meant literally, because pilots are made, not born. There's not much inherent talent needed to fly an airplane. That's why one light-plane manu-facturer advertises sample lessons for five dollars. He knows you'll find it relatively easy if you want to learn how to fly.

Stop by any small airport, and you'll find sixteen-year-old girls learning how to fly with money saved from baby-sitting jobs. I knew a couple in their sixties who were learning to-gether. I once met a man with a wooden leg who had soloed. Most student pilots are people flying in their spare time and paying for it over a long learning period.

Private flying lessons are not expensive. They can cost as little as $350, from lesson one through getting your license, depending on the type of airplane. And if it takes you a year to become fully licensed, as it did me, that averages about seven dollars a week. (Of course you can do it in a matter of weeks too.)

But you're actually flying by yourself long before that. After about eight hours of instruction, you may be allowed to solo. Following that, about half your time is spent flying by yourself, and the other half "dual," with an instructor along. After your first solo, you're issued a student's license, which allows you to fly by yourself, but doesn't permit you to take anyone with you except licensed pilots.

By far the biggest thrill is that first solo flight. It remains one of the highlights of my life, and I suspect it will for some time to come. Everything in the private pilot's course leading up to it seems merely a prelude; everything afterward becomes almost anticlimactic.

While doing the research for this book, I talked at length with many airline pilots. One day, sitting in the cockpit of a Boeing 727 jet, I asked the pilot about his biggest thrill in more than twenty years of flying.

He thought for a moment before replying, "My first solo flight. I can still remember every inch of it."

Every man in that cockpit shook his head in agreement; all had experienced the same thrill, and each man's eyes took on that dreamy reminiscent look, savoring again the sensation of flying an airplane by himself for the first time.

It's like this: Your instructor has been working with you for more than eight hours in the air, usually over a period of several weeks. For the past several days, you've been doing takeoffs and landings, takeoffs and landings, takeoffs and landings. Today, you feel, could be *the* day. Meanwhile, more takeoffs and landings. As the time approaches, the instructor remains his pedantic self. "Keep that glide speed accurate," he says softly. "Watch the runway. Stay lined up." You repeat the landing, and maybe he shoves the throttle forward, and you take off still another time. Then around in the traffic pattern, and another approach.

You're getting near-perfect on that one little exercise. The takeoffs are clean, the wings remain level; your landings are smooth three-pointers, with no bounce, and you're touching down early on the runway.

The instructor starts firing questions at you: What do you do if you encounter a sudden gust of wind? At what point do you decide to go around again? Where do you begin to flare out? You answer quickly and calmly, and you know the moment is near.

"Let me take this landing," he says unexpectedly, as you begin the umpteenth approach. "When I say go, you take

22

the stick and recover from what'll be a bad landing. O.K.?"

"O.K.," you reply, and he takes control.

He makes a good approach, but he banks sharply before touching down, and you begin to wonder if he'll ram the wing into the ground. But he's too experienced for that. It's all deliberately bad. He's going to bounce the plane off one wheel, then hand you the stick.

He does, and the jolt is resounding. You've never landed that badly!

"Take it!" he says, and you grab the stick, quickly adding a burst of power. You level out the wings and settle down into a normal landing, which looks picture-book perfect in comparison.

"Good job," comes the compliment from the other seat. "Let's do something like that again."

By now you've made maybe fifteen landings in succession. How much more do you have to take before he'll trust you to go it alone?

You start around again, beginning your neat approach. This time he deliberately flares out high, about twelve feet off the ground. Then it's all yours again.

You add a bit of power, and resume your glide down for another six or eight feet while watching the runway ahead of you, trying to estimate whether you have enough room left to land. The plane begins to settle smoothly (you're happy that he picked a smooth day), and you make the landing.

By this time, you have to taxi back in order to take off again.

"Let's do it again," the instructor says. "Only this time, *you* do it. Without me. And the right way. O.K.?"

That's the moment you've been waiting for. Solo!

You stop, holding your feet on the brakes, and let your passenger out. One more word of advice: "If you're high at all, or in any trouble, don't hesitate to go around again.

O.K.? Let's make it a good one the first time, right?"

"Right," you answer. But your voice sounds strangely shaky. You're more confident than that, aren't you?

You add power, and taxi into position. Don't forget that checklist! Check the r.p.m.'s, wiggle the control surfaces, kill one magneto at a time, try the carburetor heat. Run engine! Run smoothly, friend, and we'll stay pals. It purrs, almost as if to help you celebrate your moment of glory.

You check the final approach corridor, then the runway and the nearby taxiways. All clear. The sun shines brightly, and the road looks wide. Now taxi onto the runway. (One more glance at the panel.) Another look around: all clear. The instructor stands twenty yards away, staring. He's confident too, isn't he? Well, there was that sloppy approach you made earlier today. . . . But wait: If he weren't confident, why would he be letting you fly this thing?

One glance at the empty rear seat, to make sure. Not a soul back there. You're it. All you. All yours. He believes in you, and you believe in yourself. And in your friend the airplane. It's your machine now. Take it. It's ready to roll, the moment you throw that throttle forward. Ready?

NOW!

The plane picks up speed quickly, as you fight to hold

*A Cessna Skylane seats six and can cruise
at better than 160 m.p.h.*

*During climb-out after takeoff, nose of plane
is held down to pick up airspeed.*

the stick forward, getting the tail up off the ground. Suddenly—*too* suddenly—you're airborne. Why so quickly? Of course, you realize: Your passenger is gone. You're much lighter.

Up, up. The airspeed picks up with a sureness. The plane wants to fly. You couldn't hold it down if you tried. That engine may be turning out only 65 horsepower, but it's plenty for this airplane and its pilot.

Its pilot is you. You have to keep telling yourself that. Today you're flying. You're Mister Pilot.

Make that turn; get into the pattern. Now the carburetor heat. Now left, into the base leg. Rudder, aileron. Now left, and line up with the runway, on final. Now throttle back. Watch that airspeed. Watch it! Don't blow it. Until now it's been great; don't make a dumb mistake this late in the game!

You're lined up, and the glide speed is perfect. Down. And careful on that flare-out procedure. Easy now, eee-asy; hold it off (it's *light* without that instructor). Touch *down*.

You're home! You smile broadly, and you exhale while you're doing it.

The instructor runs over. "Great! Do it again for me, O.K.?"

"Yes, sir!"

Nothing to it this time. Back into taxi position, once again the checklist, and you're a veteran of the airways!

Back on the ground later, you're proud to keep the first-solo tradition going. Cokes for the house, on you. And in some cases, you lose a shirttail to an enthusiastic audience. Most of the hangar talk stopped while you were out there proving your mastery over the flying machine, you learn now. Everybody wanted to relive it with you, to share the glory again. Yes, sir, it's quite a thrill.

It's the moment you dreamed about. It's the occasion you had in mind when you stopped into the airport office, long ago, and asked hesitantly about flying lessons.

"I don't know the first thing about it," you said. And within minutes you were in the air, handling the controls.

Most instructors prefer it that way. After all, you came to fly, didn't you? So you get into the airplane, and somebody spins the prop for you, and you're off. The instructor says little at first. This isn't the time to burden you down with lengthy and technical information. This is your introduction to flight, and it may be that you haven't flown before.

He makes the takeoff, and you get a fright when he throttles back to normal climbing power. Then he levels the plane, and tells you to take the stick in a sweaty hand.

Now? You can't help wondering. Are you ready for this? "Not a thing to worry about," he reassures you. "I've got dual controls back here, and I'll be with you on every movement. O.K. then, let's start with straight and level flight.

"Take a good look at the nose of the airplane. See it? The airplane is level, and that's what it looks like. Appears a little off, doesn't it? Well, it's not. It's perfectly straight. Now look at both wings. Get the picture? That's what they look like straight and level. Look again at the wings and the nose. That's what we'll be coming back to after we make a slight turn here. The plane's attitude is straight and level. Remember: The *attitude* of the aircraft.

"Now we're going to experiment with the controls. The stick in your hand operates the elevators, at the rear of the plane, and also the ailerons, on the wings. If I pull it back, the elevators go up, the tail goes down, and the nose comes up. See it?"

You're deep into it, watching that nose closely. Attitude. Straight and level. Elevators. Ailerons. O.K., Instructor, talk on:

"If I move the stick left, the airplane banks left. It doesn't turn—it banks in that direction, with one wing down. Right? Watch the right wing while I move the stick left. See the aileron move down, and the wing move up? Look at the other wing. See that aileron moving up, while the right one is moving down? Together, they make the wing bank left. When I move the stick right, the left aileron moves down and the right one moves up, correct? The wing is banked right.

"Now the rudder. Those pedals under your feet actuate the rudder, on the the tail of the airplane. Right rudder pedal moves the rudder right, which makes the tail go left, and the nose go right. Got it? Left rudder pedal moves the rudder left, and the airplane left.

"To make a turn, though, I need more than the rudder. Watch what happens when I use the rudder alone. Ready?"

The plane lurches around to the left, and you feel uncomfortable for the first time in your new role as a student pilot.

"We skidded around, didn't we? That wasn't smooth at all, was it? But if you'll remember the ailerons, those things on the wings that banked the airplane, you'll recall that they don't *turn* it. To make a proper turn, we need rudder *and* aileron, in a coordinated movement. Now: Look right, apply right rudder and right aileron. See the difference? A smooth turn right. And the airplane will keep turning until you tell it to stop."

That sounds hard to believe, and you say so.

"But it's true," the instructor says. "This airplane is built to fly. It'll fly in any direction you point it. You've told it to turn, and it'll keep on turning until the engine dies of fuel starvation. To make it stop turning, apply left rudder and left aileron. Ready? Look left, check for other airplanes. Clear? O.K., left rudder, left aileron, straighten it out. Now we're straight and level again.

"Now, you take the stick and the rudder pedals, and this time I'll let go."

(You're certain you know what you're doing, Instructor? You want to get us both killed, or something?)

"Hey, hold on. Ready? O.K., I've left go. They're all yours. Hold her straight and level."

You fight the stick, trying to compensate for every twist of the nose in what started to be clear weather, but must be hurricane winds by now. Man, look at that airplane wobble!

"I must be doing something wrong . . . What do I do next?"

"O.K., you're making the simple mistake of overcontrolling the airplane. Everybody does it at first. I'll show you

28

*Cutaway model of light plane enables instructor
to demonstrate without leaving the ground.*

how to handle it. Let go of the stick and rudder pedals. Hands and feet off. Right? I'll take my hands and feet off. See?"

(The man's gone crazy!)

"It's O.K. I know what I'm doing. Don't worry. Watch the airplane. It's flying straight and level, isn't it?"

You have to admit that it is. But that's quite a trick, flying with no one at the controls.

"The airplane is designed to fly. The airspeed is making it stay in the air, and you've pointed it straight ahead, and it's responding to your orders. See it? It doesn't require any control at this point. None whatever."

(Later, you find that not exactly true, although almost. The principle, though, is driven home. You get the point.)

Now you've got the stick back again, and you resume the fight, this time struggling to resist the temptation to control every wiggle. When the plane drifts a little, you find it coming back to its starting point. When it rises slightly, or the nose drops off a bit, you discover it returning to straight and level attitude.

It's one of the hardest lessons to learn in flying. For the first several hours, you can hardly resist that impulse to correct every movement, to move that stick, and push those rudders. But you are flying now, and you are convinced in theory, if not in practice, that the airplane will fly itself.

"O.K., I think that's enough for one day. Let's head back."

The firm professional hand takes over again. "I've got it," he says in a loud voice. In the air, there should be little doubt about who's flying the airplane. Even veteran airline pilots do it that way: "I've got it."

The plane heads back home, and you're about ready for surprise number two. "Where's the airport? See it down there?"

You don't, and there's no use kidding the man. Maybe we're lost?

"Right below, see it? Look, I'll point the nose right at the runway. See it?"

Ah. One lost airport, found. It looks different from up here.

"Right. Let's bank toward our traffic pattern, and glide down." He pulls back the throttle, and the silence is deafening.

For a moment, you're certain that all power has failed, and that you're about to become a statistic. You can read the headlines: STUDENT PILOT DIES IN FIRST FLIGHT; "IN-STRUCTOR" EXPOSED AS IMPOSTOR.

But again, your fears aren't worth fearing. The engine's at idling speed, and the sharp contrast between cruising speed racket and gliding silence frightens you.

The runway gets closer, and the pilot makes minute—almost imperceptible—changes in attitude. The runway rushes up at you, and suddenly he tilts the stick back toward his lap. The nose is up, and you can't see the ground underneath you. The plane settles down, down, and touches firm earth. Once again the noise begins. The rattle of the landing gear and the vibration cut into the silence, and you know you're down.

"There, that wasn't bad, was it?"

(It certainly was. Well, maybe not as bad as I thought. But there were a few surprises, things I hadn't thought about. Yes, it was *different*, I had to admit that.)

"What? Oh, no, of course. No, it was great! Is that it? Is that the first lesson?"

"That's it, and I think you did pretty well, considering you'd never handled the controls of an airplane before. I don't think you'll have any trouble at all, once you get the hang of it. We'll spend a few minutes looking over the plane when we get out, and then I'll get you your logbook and an instruction manual, and we'll have you on your way in no time."

(Not bad, did he say? He may not know it, but I've got a long time to go before I can call myself pilot. He's no judge of ability, that's for sure.)

Now you're out, and your feet are on the ground again. You pick up the books, shake hands, make an appointment for lesson two, shake hands again, and head for the car.

Start the auto engine. Head out into traffic. Drive down the road. Look at those mortals trapped in their earthbound vehicles! They don't know what they're missing!

CHAPTER 3

The basic training of a private pilot begins with a man sitting in a machine; it concludes with a man figuratively welded to that machine, the two of them operating together.

The jiggles and jounces you experienced in your first attempt at controlling an airplane soon disappear. You don't overcontrol after a while, and the airplane—as the man said—begins to fly itself. The horizon stays steadily out there where you put it, in front of the nose, and the wings remain level. (There are tricks of the trade involved: you aim at a spot far off into the horizon, and it's easier to keep the airplane pointing in that direction. And you implant firmly in your mind the picture of a level aircraft in flight. Every maneuver you execute from then on ends with a return to that attitude.)

Following an introductory flight, you get a chance to turn and bank the airplane. Good inherent coordination helps here, although smooth maneuvering can be learned. One instructor claims that it requires less coordination to fly an airplane than it does to drive a car. He may be exaggerating, but he's on the right track; it certainly requires less constant *effort* to fly a light plane. You don't dare ease off the steering wheel of your car.

There are other things to learn as you go. The procedures for safety's sake are a big part of flying, and you learn to do them automatically. No matter how many consecutive landings and takeoffs you make, for example, you always perform a run-up before each takeoff. You taxi to a spot near the runway, and push the throttle forward until you're getting 1500 r.p.m.'s from the recording tachometer. Then you cut out one magneto at a time (the airplane has a dual magneto system), and make certain that the r.p.m.'s remain fairly constant. Next you pull out the carburetor heat knob; the r.p.m.'s should drop slightly. You check to make sure that the ailerons, elevators, and rudder are responding to the controls. Next comes a quick check of all instruments. Is there enough fuel? Is the altimeter set properly? Is everything else in working order?

Most trouble can be spotted before you get in the airplane or before you take off. It's certainly the proper time to spot troubles. Few pilots would want to wait until midflight.

My own first thirty minutes of logged time was spent in an introduction flight. My logbook (it's dated back to 1956) reads something like this:

Run-up, St. & Level, Turns	40 min.
Coordination, St. & Level Flight	40 min.
Climbs, Glides, Slo Flight, 90°, 180°, 360° Turns	45 min.
St. & Level Turns, Climb & Gliding Turns	1 hr.
Stalls, 720's, Glides, Climbs	30 min.

So that after three hours and thirty-five minutes in the air, I had experienced most of the very basic maneuvers. Making a turn is one thing; making it while climbing or gliding is something else again.

The "slo flight" entry in my log refers to a method of slowing the airplane down to almost minimum controllable speed. It's used in rough weather primarily, and can be a handy thing to know. It also helps because it's learned before the student gets into stalling, which is a word he'll hear often in flying.

A stall does not mean that the engine stops. It means,

aerodynamically, that the airplane is no longer maintaining enough speed (lift) to fly. If you're moseying along at cruising speed in a light plane, and suddenly begin hauling back on the stick, the nose rises and the airspeed drops. The light planes aren't meant to fly straight up, and they won't. What happens is that the airspeed over the wings is decreased until all lift has disappeared. When that point is reached, the airplane is no longer flying; it is falling through the air.

Each airplane has its own stalling speed—the speed at which it will stall—and the pilot must know what it is. He also must know how to handle a stall if one should occur. There's nothing frightening about stalling, but there is something frightening about not knowing what to do next. And so the fledgling pilot gets well acquainted with stalls. He learns what the airplane "feels" like just before it stalls (the controls get suddenly mushy, and ineffectual). He learns to anticipate the stall itself (the nose drops suddenly), and he learns to leave the ailerons alone in the stall, to straighten the airplane out with the rudder, to let it dive a few feet until airspeed is regained. The whole stall is over in a matter of seconds. Properly learned, you lose maybe fifty feet of altitude in executing one.

Surprisingly, the stall can occur in any flight attitude. It can happen in a high-speed turn (when the stalling speed is greatly increased, proportionate to the degree of the turn); it can happen in a glide, a climb, or in straight and level flight. And another surprise: the stalling speed changes, depending on factors like the weight of the plane, and the altitude at which you're flying.

The biggest surprise is that *part of the airplane stalls before the rest of it does*. What you expect isn't necessarily what happens. In a stall that occurs while in a severe bank and turn, for example, the airplane reacts exactly the opposite from what you expect. If you're turning left and banking sharply in that direction, it seems that a stall would

A pilot in a Cessna Skymaster,
with counter-rotating props, practices stalls.

make that left wing drop, and that you would plunge in that direction. It doesn't. The right wing drops, because the left wing, on the inside of the turn, is actually moving faster than the right wing, on the outside of the turn. Since what you're concerned about is airspeed over the surface of the wing (which produces lift), it's understandable that the airspeed drops first on the slower wing. The plane stalls from right to left. And when the right wing loses life, it goes down.

You learn that stalls can easily become spins, which are worth avoiding. But even though the course doesn't require that you spin the airplane (it used to), it does cover the procedure for recovering from an inadvertent spin. It also includes other safety-first procedures, such as crosswind landings, forced landings, and short-field takeoffs.

Throughout, the emphasis is on handling the plane with safety in mind. One newly graduated pilot was heard to remark that "I may not be good, but at least I'm safe." He was right. Every new pilot has had that kind of training; nobody can avoid it. The instructor suddenly cuts the engine back to idle while you're still a mile from the field, at 2,000 feet. It's your job to glide properly into a safe landing approach, facing the right way.

If safety is the overriding skill, however, then coordination is a close cousin. The course is designed to make you part of the machine, or to make the machine part of you.

"When those wings out there begin to feel like extensions of your arms," says one veteran instructor, "you're beginning to think like a pilot."

Making the man-machine work together requires hours of practice. The landing, for instance, is attempted only after the student has covered the danger areas (stalls, etc.) plus the routine gliding and gliding turns, rectangular-course flying, and something the handbook calls S turns.

The S turn practice helps develop all the areas of needed coordination. You pick a spot over a road, or hedgerow, and —at 600 feet— fly in an S-shaped pattern across it. Actually, the S is more like a figure 8, since you make the same turns over and over again. The idea is to maintain perfectly your altitude (within 25 feet), while flying exactly perpendicular to the road every time you cross it. The first time I tried it I found myself at everything but right angles to the road. It took me twenty minutes of practice before I could get the airplane to do what I wanted it to, and another hour before I could do it consistently. From then on, I practiced S turns by the hour, whenever I could.

Takeoffs and landings come next, and almost invariably prove to be much more difficult than they look.

The one thing my instructor missed (at least in my case) was the amount of play in the rudder pedals. He may have told me, but either he or I forgot that important item when it came time for my first takeoff. The result was that I almost plowed corn that day.

36

We went through the taxiing procedure, and found ourselves on the end of the runway. On the ground, the rudders are loose to the touch. To get any kind of response out of the airplane, you have to floor one of the rudder pedals. After you get some decent airspeed over the rudder, a light touch will produce a turn. I'd been so used to that light touch that I forgot how "sloppy" the rudders felt on the ground.

My takeoff runway ran next to a cornfield, and when it was time to go I pushed the old throttle like a pro. As per instructions, I pushed the stick forward (to raise the tail off the ground) in the Aeronca Champion. There I was, slowly picking up airspeed, bumping along on the main two wheels, expecting that a feather-light rudder push would keep me lined up on the runway.

The plane drifted right, and I applied a dainty little toe push to the left rudder pedal. Nothing. More drift right, and another toe touch. Still nothing. By this time we were on the extreme right-hand side of the runway, with maybe five yards remaining between us and the cornfield.

"Give her some left rudder," said my instructor.

"That's what I'm trying to do," I shouted over the roar of the engine. "She doesn't want to go left."

Now we had inches left. Fortunately, we were almost off the ground. More touches, and still no response.

Suddenly I heard the instructor's voice, authoritatively: "I've got it." I gladly relinquished the controls to the pro in the seat behind me.

He moved left smoothly, and at just that moment we were airborne—right over the adjacent cornfield.

We turned around and landed. And it was then that he explained to me about rudder pressure, sounding like a patient kindergarten teacher with a five-year-old who couldn't keep the sand in the sandbox.

From that first takeoff on, I've always kept my feet jammed hard against the rudder pedals on takeoff. And I don't think I've wavered more than a few feet from the center line of the runway since.

Altogether, according to my original frayed logbook, I spent more than five hours before solo landing and taking off with an instructor in the airplane. Conservatively figuring, that must have been at least fifty landings and takeoffs, over a five-week period. By the time I soloed, I was beginning to feel that the wheels were an extension of my feet.

Takeoffs have always seemed more dangerous to me than landings. Given the proper airspeed and altitude for a good landing approach, you've got to come down. Once I've set up that glide, pointing at the runway with a little altitude to spare, I've never worried about landing. I *know* I'm going to reach the runway safely, and it's merely a case of touching down.

The takeoff, though, is something else again. I'm applying power, trying to get up in the air within a specified distance (there's only so much runway). What happens if my engine should quit after I reached, say, 100 feet of altitude? The book says, and I believe it, that the only thing to do is keep the airplane pointing straight ahead. A sharp turn can be disastrous at that low altitude, and the odds are that you'll never be able to make it back to the same runway. Stalling speed is raised, and you aren't moving too fast to start with.

It all comes down to how reliable the engine is. Mine have been perfect, and for that matter, I've never known one to quit suddenly. It's understandable when you think about it. How many times have you known a perfectly good auto engine to quit suddenly—with absolutely no warning—when you're driving down a highway? And in the few times that I've heard of it happening in a car, I've always discovered that somebody hadn't checked the oil level for a week, or hadn't changed sparkplugs in two years, or something as foolish.

Airplane engines are checked with tedious regularity, and you run-up before you start your takeoff. Always. The idea is to have the engine running at its best every time, with no exceptions. I've taken off from fields with power lines at the end of the runway, and with barns and busy highways. I'd hate to think of the consequences had the engine decided to stop.

I was greatly relieved to read a Cessna advertisement once that told of an airplane staying aloft for several days. The little engine kept purring along through it all. I was convinced then that I was flying with something dependable in front of me.

I was at an airport once when a man landed a rented plane and complained about a "strange noise" in the air. Mechanics swarmed over that airplane, and the flight instructor checked out every instrument. They didn't stop there, either. There was no logical reason for the noise, and so they test-flew it. An instructor and a mechanic taxied it out to a runway, and took off. The "malfunction" turned out to be the visiting pilot's Thermos bottle, rattling around in the glove compartment.

It was a comforting feeling to see those people so concerned about one little unidentified noise. Especially since I was the guy who had to fly that same airplane next.

CHAPTER 4

Postsolo instruction is the point at which you get the lean meat of flying experience. It is the time when you hone your skills, aiming for the day when a certified FAA examiner looks you over and decides whether you can be trusted to take people into the air.

It surprised me to learn that the first thing I had to do after my solo—after all those takeoffs and landings to prepare for that big day—was to practice more takeoffs and landings. And I had to be checked out. My instructor went along while I made three more sets of takeoffs and landings, then left me while I spent forty minutes more in practice. Two weeks later I was back at the same routine again, and it was at this point that I realized the truth in the instructor's words, "Every landing is different."

They're all different, just as every air current is distinct. Getting into a standard landing pattern involves flying the downwind leg (parallel to the runway, but in the opposite direction), then the base leg (at a right angle to the runway), then the final approach, heading for the target runway. If you turn onto the base leg five feet shorter than your last turn, the chances are that you'll make a different landing; at least you'll probably touch down on a different spot along the runway. And how many people do you think can slice through a particular chunk of air at exactly the same speed and altitude every time? To complicate matters even more, the two runways at the Bethlehem-Easton Airport both had high obstructions. You had to fly over them to get down on either one.

I found myself touching down on the first fifty feet of runway one time, and the first two hundred feet another time.

If runway length is protection against accidents, then it makes sense to have as much runway in front of you as possible. (On takeoffs you always use every available foot—just in case.) So the objective was to touch down as early as possible, leaving plenty of room for coming to a stop. One of the runways was about 2,400 feet in length at the Bethlehem-Easton Airport, and the other was a little shorter. I used both, coming in from both ends, and finally reached the stage where I could be fairly consistent about touching down, in any of the four directions.

But before I got to that point in my training, I had used up another four and a quarter hours of flight time. I had almost fourteen hours' experience in the air by now, and felt confident about landing *this particular airplane on this particular field.*

Part of my training at this juncture was to practice side-slips. By crossing the controls (*right* aileron, *left* rudder—or vice versa), you can "slip" the airplane down quickly while using up a little runway length. This technique helps if you're going into a short field, or if you have to clear a high barrier at the end of the runway, such as a power line, or if you have too much altitude and you want to lose it in a hurry. It's a tricky maneuver, and in my own naïve way I managed to perfect it in the Aeronca without realizing how potentially dangerous it could be. You have to keep the nose down by keeping the stick forward, or risk a low-altitude stall.

On one of these solo days, I proudly asked a Navy pilot to join me for a short hop and a demonstration of my new skills. He sat in the back seat while I made a fifteen-minute circuit of the immediate area and got back into the landing pattern, deliberately coming in a little high. I began the sideslip, concentrating on my work, and was doing nicely until he began worrying aloud.

"Careful, Ed, careful!" he kept repeating. We came out of it nicely, and landed beautifully, and I beamed a naïve smile. "What were you so worried about?" I asked.

"Well, it's been years since I've done anything like that," he confessed. "I know it's standard procedure in light planes, but it still doesn't *seem* right. I mean coming so close to a stall." He managed a rather weak smile, but he declined my offer to try it again.

It was on that same day that my instructor invited me to ride with him in a Cessna 172, a four-place vinyl-interior airplane with all the comforts, including a cigarette lighter. His job was to take two passengers on a short sight-seeing flight, and he asked me if I'd like to go along, riding in the right-hand front seat with him.

This was the same instructor who taught me sideslips, and the same instructor who later pointed out the intricacies of high-speed stalls and other maneuvers. For some reason, he made his approach slightly high when we returned from that hop. But instead of sideslipping, he waited it out and landed farther down the runway. When we had parked, I asked him why.

"Never subject a passenger to anything unnecessarily," he said. "The passenger wants to fly, not get scared half to death. Aviation has lost a lot of potential customers because of hotshot pilots showing off. I'm not here to scare off potential customers, and neither are you."

It was the last time I've ever done anything more exciting than I had to in the air—with or without passengers.

We practiced crosswind landings next. The trick is to lower a wing into the wind, to keep from being blown off course, and to point the ship as much as possible into the wind while approaching the runway.

Then we covered "wheel landings," which are used in strong winds. You add more power, and touch down on the front two wheels only.

Soon afterward, I was ready for cross-country flying. My first cross-country trip was made dual, with an instructor sitting along for the ride. We talked about everything but flying that day, as I made a successful 100-mile round trip.

The trickiest thing about cross-country flying in a plane with no radio is finding your way. You may be pointing at a proper heading, say 240 degrees on the magnetic compass, but a little wind can carry you miles off your course unless you correct for it. So you pick out a nearby spot on the aeronautical chart, aim to cross directly over it, and see where the wind takes you. Then you make corrections as you go. Maybe you have to steer an indicated course of 250 degrees in order to stay on an actual 240-degree heading.

On one trip, I was blown two miles off course within a ten-mile segment; I learned to pay attention to drift after that.

Most small airports don't have control towers. A few have a private pilot's radio frequency (called Unicom), but it is seldom used by many fledgling pilots simply because they have no transmitting equipment. So you decide which runway to use by making visual contact with the ground. You check smokestacks if you can, and determine which way the wind is blowing. Or you wait until you reach the airport proper, and take a long hard look at the wind sock; you take off and land into the wind, into the small end of the wind sock.

I made one practice approach downwind one day, and found myself landing twenty miles an hour faster than I expected.

Runways are numbered according to compass headings. Thus a runway pointing directly west would always be numbered 27, shorthand for 270 degrees, or due west, on the compass. The same runway, used in the opposite direction, would be number 9, short for 90 degrees, or due east. One pointing south would be number 18, and one due north would be 36. Many runways are between major points on the compass; they are numbered according to the exact direction in which they point, such as 22 for 220°, and 4 for 40°

It is not easy for the neophyte who is looking for a proper approach into a landing pattern at a strange airport. The pattern is usually set up resembling a rectangle, and you approach the active runway from the left. (Although right-hand patterns are used too, and many airports with control towers authorize straight-in approaches when they can be used.) To get into a pattern, you first have to determine which runway is in use. If you're approaching the field from the west, on a heading of 90°, you must first determine if (let's say) Runway 18 is being used. Your first step would be to get south of the airport and circle left, so that you'd be flying due north at 600 feet, paralleling Runway 18, which faces due south. You'd be on a downwind leg for Runway 18.

After reaching the end of the field, say a half mile past the end of the runway, you'd make a 90° turn left. At that point you'd be flying at a right angle to the runway, and you'd be on the base leg. Next you turn to face 18, coming out of the turn in time to line up with the runway. And you've already begun your glide down for a landing at that point.

One of the ticklish parts of the landing itself involves the glide, or the attitude of the aircraft as it approaches the runway. The gliding speed has to be kept considerably higher than stalling speed, in order to allow for a safety margin. And it has to be slow enough to let you flatten out the attitude quickly, and get the airplane down on the ground.

In the old Aeronca Champion, the gliding speed was 65 miles per hour. (The Champion cruised at 85, and stalled at about 40). To maintain the gliding speed, you manipulated the control stick. If the plane drifted up near 70 m.p.h., you pulled back on the stick, raising the nose and making it slow down. If it got slow, you lowered the nose by edging the stick forward, thereby picking up more airspeed.

If your airspeed was satisfactory but your glide was too steep, you edged the throttle forward in order to raise the nose a little and flatten out the glide.

In simpler terms, airspeed is controlled by the stick, and the airplane's angle of attack is controlled with the throttle.

Coming in on final approach, you watch not only the path of your glide, and your alignment with the runway, but also your airspeed indicator. If you have to raise the nose in order to clear an obstacle at the end of the field, you add throttle; if your airspeed is off, you adjust it by using the stick. The trickiest thing here is to coordinate the two —while keeping the airplane lined up for a landing.

Most instructors teach it in small stages. First you learn how to set up a glide, at the proper speed, and how to maintain it. Then you learn how to control the angle of glide by adding and reducing power. Then you put both of them together for a proper landing approach.

Next comes the technique of flaring out for a landing. Ideally, you're in a rather shallow glide as you cross the threshold of the runway, running at exactly the proper speed. But since stalling speed (the same as landing speed)

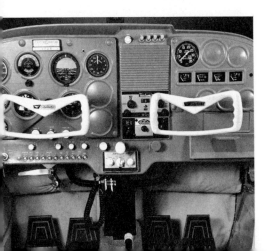

*The panel
of a modern
light plane*

is considerably lower than your gliding speed, you have to get rid of the excess somehow.

Say you're gliding at 65 m.p.h., and that the plane stalls at 40. That means that 25 m.p.h. of speed is going to have to be dissipated somehow before the plane will settle onto the ground and stay down. So you flare (flatten the glide) and ride parallel to the runway just before touchdown. The secret is to look out ahead of the plane, and not straight down at the ground. In this way, you get some perspective that will show you where you are in relation to the ground.

A few feet above the runway, you ease back (gently!) on the stick. The plane loses airspeed and begins to settle after a moment or two. Then you ease back more, and more, trying to hold it off the ground. The more you ease back, the more speed you lose. Gradually you drop the whole 25 m.p.h., and the plane stalls (settles) right on the runway. If you do it right, all three wheels touch down at the same time. And at that moment, the stick should be far back in your lap.

Sounds easy? It is, relatively speaking. But you have to get the feel of it first. One instructor I know doesn't let his students try flaring out until they've mastered the approach glide. His theory is that glide is tricky enough for beginners, without throwing in the final landing techniques.

And one gust of wind can create near havoc in the beginner's mind. A gust from the left can blow that little fabric-covered airplane far to the right, and you have to compensate by leaning the left wing into the wind. And when you touch down in a windy situation like that one, the airplane has a tendency to head immediately into the wind. It sometimes requires fairly hard rudder pressure to keep it aligned.

All those techniques are required in normal landings. But some landings aren't normal at all. A strong, steady crosswind, for example, can create a situation requiring skillful maneuvering. In that case, the wing must be kept down into the wind during the entire final part of the landing. And before that, you'll have to "crab" the airplane—head the nose into the wind and let the plane fly sideways toward its target down the runway. Crabbing is a normal procedure during a cruise in a crosswind. But it gets extra tricky on final approach. The secret is to straighten it out before the touchdown, and to align with the windward side of the runway, in case you get blown a few feet off your target.

A strong headwind is still another problem. Whenever possible, of course, the active runway will be one that heads directly into the face of the wind. If a strong wind is blowing directly from the west, you can be sure that Runway 27 is it. Providing that there *is* a Runway 27. Some airports aren't laid out that way. You might find yourself landing on Runway 32 or Runway 22; either way, you've got a crosswind to contend with.

But if the wind is directly down the runway, and strong, still another type of landing is required. This one is called a power landing, or wheel landing. You come in with more power, and fly the airplane down onto the runway, instead of letting it settle. The stall occurs on the ground, and isn't perceptible. It's somewhat difficult to learn, because you push the stick forward when you touch down, instead of easing it back. And at this point in your instructions you find it hard to break that new habit of pulling back on the stick.

The first time I tried a wheel landing I was certain we were going to scrape the propellor along the ground, and tip over. It's that kind of sensation. My reaction was to hold the stick fairly steady, and my instructor had to force it forward. We had to spend half an hour on wheel landings before I began to feel competent.

A few other maneuvers are musts. One is called the seven-twenty, short for a 720° turn, or two complete 360° circles. I struggled with that turn (which must be precise) for a long time before I learned a trick that made it easier. One of the older students at little Bethlehem-Easton Airport told me about the trick one day while we were sipping soda in the hangar.

"Before you start your turn, look carefully at the shadows inside the cockpit," he said. (The latticelike bracing inside the Champ did create several shadows across the panel.) "Come out of the turn in time to put those shadows back where they were to start off with."

I tried it the next afternoon, and made several precise turns in a row. "Great improvement over yesterday," said my instructor. I thought I had him fooled. But later, when I told him what I was doing, he agreed that it was a good technique. After I'd learned precision turns like that, it was an easy transition to making them off the compass instead of the shadows. Besides, you may find yourself flying on cloudy days.

The latter part of the private pilot's course contains cross-country flights of several hundred miles. You make the first one dual, and the second and third solo. The object is simple enough: prove that you can take the airplane somewhere and get it back in one piece without getting lost.

Getting lost! I can't think of anything that's easier to do in a radioless airplane. Or even one with radio, for that matter. The ground all looks alike to most neophyte fliers, and—contrary to what you see on most maps—the states don't have distinct colors. You can drift across state lines without once encountering that large maplike lettering "Michigan" or "New Jersey." It's all up to you, and how well you can read aeronautical charts. The chart shows you everything you need to know. It pinpoints the location of towers, mountain peaks, railroads, high tension lines, mine pits, rivers, and airports. Towns on the map are shaped to conform with the actual shape below you. Airways, the "roads" that professional pilots follow, are clearly marked. And so are all the ground radio facilities. The chart tells you a lot about individual airports; how many runways they have, the length of the longest one, and the tower radio frequencies. But it doesn't necessarily keep you from getting lost!

I don't know of one student pilot who ever completed his course without getting disoriented at least once. One instructor says that you're not a pilot until you've been lost. (In that case, it's easy enough to become a pilot.)

CHAPTER 5

The first cross-country flight is usually about 100 miles. I made it with instructor Jim Frankenfield to Hershey, Pennsylvania, near Harrisburg. All the students at the Bethlehem-Easton Airport used the Hershey runway; the staff picked it out because it's one airport that's relatively easy to find. We had a completely uneventful trip. There was some wind, but I watched the checkpoints carefully on the ground, and crabbed into the wind in order to compensate for it. I was on a perfect course within five minutes after leaving the ground, and we had a pleasant ride over and back.

Jim kept chatting away in the back seat about the things a pilot must do when he's in the air. The two prime responsibilities: stay on course, and watch out for other airplanes. Several times he spotted other planes in the sky, usually far below or above us, or off to one side. "Traffic at 9 o'clock low," he'd say, and I'd spend the next few moments trying to confirm his spot. Like most of flying, there's a trick to spotting airplanes. Glancing around quickly isn't the way to find them. The best method is to look off in one direction for a few seconds, letting your peripheral vision pick up anything that's moving within your scope of vision. Then look off in another direction, and another, and another— varying the directions sharply. I became good enough after a while to spot them before Jim did, and I was the one who was doing the flying. All he had to do was sit back of me and look.

Carburetor icing is another problem. Ice can form in the carburetor under widely differing climatic conditions—especially on warm, humid days.

That's what the carburetor heat control is for: it forces warm air into the carburetor and prevents (or destroys) ice. The carb heat is pulled out on every landing, and occasionally on long trips to make certain that the carburetor is staying free of ice. Since ice can cause engine failure, it's a good idea to use the little gadget.

I had an icing situation on my return trip to Hershey, flying solo. I noticed the r.p.m.'s dropping off, and I immediately suspected ice. Sure enough, adding carb heat created a louder engine sound which I knew was proof of icing. I kept it on for most of the trip, to make sure. (It's not kept on normally, because it decreases engine power and cuts down cruising speed.)

This second Hershey trip was smooth all the way with the exception of that icing condition. And so was my third cross-country flight, to Glens Falls, New York. Halfway there, another light plane passed me on my left, no more than fifty yards away. It was an old Taylorcraft, and his cruising speed made my 85 m.p.h. look like a crawl; he and his wife waved as they went by, and later I chatted with them at Glens Falls. He had just purchased the four-lace T-Craft, and he had only 100 hours in the air. It was the first trip he had made with his wife. "Beautiful," she kept saying. "Flying is wonderful." And her husband, beaming with pride, smiled broadly.

I didn't tell them that flying solo in an unheated airplane in November could be mighty unbeautiful at times.

The days were getting shorter and chillier, and I was approaching the end of the private course. We spent most of our time going over maneuvers I had already learned, and landing at a nearby larger airport with paved runways

—which seemed like pillows after the turf landings at the Bethlehem-Easton Airport.

I took the private pilot's written exam at that same airport. For weeks before, I had been studying every question and answer in the instruction book. I wasn't overconfident, but I did make a perfect score on that test. (Soon afterward, they changed the test and included much more complicated problems. I'm not sure what I would have scored on the new one, but I know it wouldn't have been 100.)

Now only two things remained before I got my private license, and they both were given by Eugene Trigiani. Gene, a qualified FAA examiner as well as an instructor, was required to give me a two-part flying exam, one in flying proficiency itself and the other in cross-country navigation.

I'm basically nervous, and I guess I showed it when we took off for the first test. "Relax," Gene kept saying. "I'm not trying to flunk you, I'm trying to determine whether you can fly safely. I know you can; all you have to do is demonstrate it for me."

And so we did short-field takeoffs and landings, wheel landings, high-speed stalls, precise turns, and "forced" landings, in addition to a dozen other maneuvers. I scored high despite my nervousness, and I started to feel more confident about the second part of the test, scheduled for the following day. But I needed more than confidence.

"Plan a trip to Newark, New Jersey," Gene said. And I had to plot the course, the weather, the anticipated fuel consumption, exact flying time, etc. When he was satisfied with my planning, we took off.

We flew just ten minutes, though, before he switched it all abruptly. "I changed my mind," he said suddenly. "I want to go to Albany, New York."

I was sure I had flunked it, and I guess my expression gave me away. Jim Frankenfield came by, and asked me what had happened. I told him. "No sweat," he said. "You knew about where you were, and you were able to return safely. He's got to pass you. You're safe, and that's what counts. Everybody gets lost, and that's a nasty little trick Gene has, insisting on an abrupt switch in flight plans, when you've set up your course to the original destination. But it's his way of testing you to make sure you can find your way back. That's the important thing. Sure, you would have scored higher had you been able to set up an immediate course to Albany. But he won't fail you because you didn't. Wait and see."

Jim sounded convincing, and I finally got up enough nerve to walk into the office. I opened the door, expecting silence.

"CONGRATULATIONS!"

The noise reverberated around the tiny shack. Gene and everybody else in the shack were shouting at the top of their lungs. "Good job," Gene said, smiling. "And now the real learning begins. You've got your private license. It's up to you to see that you continue to learn. I think you've proved to yourself today that you still have a way to go before you become the perfect pilot."

I paid for the Cokes, and everybody guzzled happily. Forty-four hours and ten minutes flying time after I got into that Champ for the first time, I was a licensed private pilot.

CHAPTER 6

Even though I'd flown as a passenger in the beautiful new Cessna 172 owned by Gene, I didn't begin to appreciate it until I flew it myself. The four-place Cessna was equipped with heater, sun visors, and a cigarette lighter. It had two fuel tanks instead of one, and soft vinyl upholstery. Best of all, the dual controls were side by side, instead of tandem. And you sat high enough to see well in front of the airplane.

It had a tricycle landing gear (a nosewheel instead of a tail wheel), and taxiing was easy. You could see!

But the most distinct difference was in the handling of the plane. This one had flaps that extended down a full 40 degrees from the wing, slowing the plane for a landing around 60 m.p.h., though the cruising speed was 110.

"It's the same principle," said Jim Frankenfield, as we took off with me at the controls of the 172 for the first time. "The only difference is that things happen faster than in the Champ." He was right. Especially on landings. It took a while to make the transition; two hours and forty-five minutes later I was ready to solo the 172 for the first time. And "Cessna Five Eight Seven Two Alpha" and I became good friends after that. I made so many trips in that 172 I can still remember the call letters without looking them up in my logbook. It was the airplane in which I learned about radio procedures, and the airplane in which I learned about radio navigation.

*The Skyknight has a cruising range
of more than 800 miles.*

I'd heard the word "omni" many times before, but I had
no idea what the gadget could do until I began flying the
Cessna. Omni is shorthand for very high frequency omni-
range navigation. The omni set in your plane is a radio re-
ceiver which enables you to home in on a station and let
its signals lead you there—or away from it. There are omni
stations all across the country, each one broadcasting signals
a full 360 degrees around it. You tune in the station, set
your course heading toward it, and keep a little needle centered in a gauge. That's basically all there is to it; if you drift
left, away from the signal, the needle drifts right. You correct your course accordingly, and not even strong crosswinds
can carry you off course. Not only that: a signal flag tells
you "to" or "from"—whether you're heading toward the
station or away from it.

And there's another advantage. By tuning in another station off to one side, and making some quick calculations, you can determine your true ground speed. That in turn enables you to estimate accurately your time of arrival. I demonstrated it once for a friend, on the way to Utica, New York. "We'll be over Utica at 3:12," I predicted at 2:40. At exactly 3:12 we crossed the omni station below.

(Airspeed is the speed at which the airplane is moving through the air. Ground speed is the speed at which it's passing over the ground. Sometimes there can be quite a difference between the two. You may be cruising at 100 m.p.h., but a 20-mile tail wind will mean that you're passing over the ground at 120 m.p.h. And a 20-mile head wind means you're doing 80 over the ground. It can make quite a difference in landing. If your normal landing speed is 60, and you're landing into a 20-mile wind, you touch down at 40. One pilot I know tells of a time when the Navy's basic trainers at Pensacola Naval Air Station in Florida could hardly land because of the wind. Their landing speed was about 60 miles an hour, and the wind came up in gusts to well over 50. Crewmen had to run alongside the crawling airplanes and hold down the wings during the landing.)

With the omni system, finding your way becomes easy. You can use adjacent stations to determine exactly where you are. And that's a handy system, especially for a novice pilot who was bred on radioless Champs.

Your new skills with radio are a pleasure to use. The Government has radio facilities spread from coast to coast, and they're in business to help the pilot, whether he's flying a commercial jet or a fighter or a single-seater for pleasure. They'll give you weather forecasts, conditions en route, traffic information, and anything else they can offer. And it's free. File a flight plan and they'll check on you every step of the way. Call them in a busy commercial area, and they'll identify you by radar, and steer you away from other airplanes in the vicinity.

Look in on a typical pleasure cruise to get some idea of

the services they offer to the airman:

Say we're flying from Whitford Airport, west of Syracuse, New York, to Raquette Lake seaplane base in the Adirondack Mountains so that your friend, who is thinking of buying a seaplane, can take a look at the area. Your land-based plane can't land there, so you have to plan to make the round trip. In your early model 172, however, the 30-plus-gallon fuel capacity is plenty for this round trip of about 220 miles.

Your first step is to check the nearest FAA station for a complete weather rundown on the area. As a private pilot without an instrument rating, you're allowed to fly only if the ceiling is above 1,000 feet, and the visibility more than three miles. (You're flying VFR—visual flight rules.) But you picked a near-perfect day for this trip: there are some scattered clouds at 12,000 feet, and the visibility is better than twenty miles. Next you plot the trip, using the Albany sectional chart published by the U.S. Coast and Geodetic Survey of the Department of Commerce. It contains the information you'll need to plan an accurate route.

You draw a straight line between Whitford and Raquette Lake, and your plastic plotter tells you the distance is about 110 miles—exactly 60 minutes' flying time in your Cessna. Align the plotter correctly on the chart, and you learn that the magnetic compass heading to Raquette is 61 degrees—northeast from your starting point. But now you have to add a little to that heading, because magnetic compasses are incorrect; in this area (according to the chart), you'll have to add 12 degrees to that heading to get a correct course. That makes your new heading 73°.

The wind is light and variable today, less than 5 m.p.h., and probably will have little effect on your trip. It also means that almost any runway will do for takeoff, and you notice that the planes at Whitford are using Runway 9, toward the east. That means you'll have to make a left turn after you leave the pattern (turning from 90° to 73°).

In twenty minutes, you're finished plotting the trip. Estimated fuel consumption, 20 gallons (leaving enough for a spare hour or more in the air, if necessary).

Your takeoff time is 11 A.M., and you expect to arrive over Raquette at noon, spend maybe ten minutes flying around the area, and arrive back before 1:15 P.M.

Now, with chart handy and radio frequencies jotted down, it's time to preflight the aircraft. The check is necessary; although the plane's been flown recently, and checked out thoroughly, little things can go wrong. This is the time to find them. You'll want to see that the control surfaces are clean, and that the propeller is free from heavy nicks or cracks. Ten minutes later, at 10:50 A.M., it's time to board the Cessna.

Check to see that your passengers fasten their seat belts, and that all doors are securely closed. Before starting the engine, take a thorough look around the airplane. Everybody away? In a loud voice, you say, "Clear!" Turn the electric starter over, and let the engine catch. Quick now: sweep over the instrument panel to see that oil pressure is registering, and that other vital gauges are giving you the right information.

Feet off the brakes, and add a little throttle to begin taxiing. The control wheel (called the yoke) is pulled back toward you; you steer by using the rudder pedals to turn the nose gear.

Out near the runway, you perform the run-up check by revving the plane up to 1500 r.p.m.'s. Everything checks out. You wiggle the wheel and rudder pedals to see that you've got free movement. With the traffic pattern clear and the runway free of other airplanes, it's time to go.

Since Whitford is 390 feet above sea level, you'll want to set your altimeter at 390 feet. And you'll be taking off from Runway 9, which means that you'll preset your gyrocompass at 90°.

Taxi the Cessna into position and slowly push in the

throttle. The plane bumps down the turf runway, begins to feel lighter, and you can feel it beginning to lift. Ease back on the stick, and—you're flying. Hold the wheel somewhat forward until you've picked up sufficient airspeed. Ease back again, and watch it go. Pull the switch on the gyrocompass, and it tells you accurately what your heading is.

Throttle back, and climb out at 90 m.p.h. to your altitude, which in this case will be a predetermined 4500 feet. Turn to a heading of 73°. At 4400 feet, you begin to throttle back still farther, until your tachometer shows 2350 r.p.m.'s—your cruising speed. Level off at 4500. The airspeed indicator shows 110 m.p.h., and you know it's quite accurate, because there's so little breeze today.

Now it's time to use your radio. Pick out the frequency, 117.0, for Syracuse Radio. Tell them you want to file a VFR flight plan. They'll want to know what kind of radio equipment you have, how many passengers you're carrying, what model airplane it is, and what time you expect to arrive at your destination. Explain carefully that you won't be landing at Raquette Lake, but overflying it and then returning. Tell them that you'll check in when you arrive.

Get ready to use that omni set in your panel. The Syracuse Omni station is located northwest of Whitford, and a heading (outbound radial) from it to Raquette is also 73°. You have a choice here: You can fly in a direct line to Raquette, using Syracuse Omni as a guide, or you can intercept that outbound radial and fly it. That's somewhat longer, and so you elect to take the direct path, saving a few minutes en route.

Tune in Syracuse Omni. You'll identify it by its repeating Morse Code signal: dit-dit-dit, DAH-dit-DAH-DAH, dit-DAH-dit, for SYR, which is also printed on your chart. Spin the course selector until it reads 73°, and watch the needle lean over to the right-hand side of the gauge, and the flag which reads "FROM." The set is telling you that you'll have to fly right in order to intercept that 73° radial. But you already know that; your chart shows you that the radial will intercept your own course before you reach Raquette. If you're correct, the needle will begin to drift left, toward the center of the dial, as you fly farther on. When it is centered, you're right on the radial. So your job here is to fly an accurate 73° course.

You will have spotted several landmarks below you. The chart shows that you'll pass to the left of the village of Belgium, crossing first a river and then a transmission line. Your course also takes you directly over Brewertown, and over the extreme western portion of Oneida Lake. You'll want to watch carefully at this point, because you may be off by a degree or two in your heading, and every mile you travel will carry you that much farther away from your intended course. The plane should be flying exactly where the line on the chart indicates.

Now is an excellent time to check your ground speed, and see what effect the wind is having on you, if any. Make certain of your course first: right on 73°, the omni needle still pointing right, and the checkpoints coming up below with precision.

Tune in to Watertown Omni, some fifty miles to the north. Draw a line from Watertown south, across your intended course. The chart shows you that your drawn line is on a Watertown radial of 185°. Draw another line, following the 170° radial from Watertown—also intersecting your course. Now you measure the distance from the point of the first intersection to the second: exactly twelve miles. Keep that figure in mind. Meanwhile, tuned to Watertown Omni, pick out a course of 185° and watch the needle carefully. At any minute, it will center itself on the dial, and then, you'll want to look at the sweep second hand on your watch.

Next, pick out the 170° radial from Watertown, and

watch the needle again. When it's centered, check the watch again. You've intercepted that radial, and traveled precisely twelve miles along your course. It took exactly six minutes. That's the piece of information you wanted. Twelve ground miles covered, in six minutes, is 120 m.p.h. Your ground speed is 10 m.p.h. faster than your indicated airspeed. In short, you have a ten-mile tailwind. (Remember that: it'll be a headwind on the way back, and it'll cut your ground speed to 100 m.p.h.)

You'll have to alter your estimated time of arrival over Raquette now; at this rate, you'll cover the 110 miles in 55 minutes, arriving five minutes early.

Ahead of you is another problem. The chart designated a specific area across your course as a military climb corridor. Where you cross it, at 4500 feet, you can expect jets to be flying between the altitudes of 10,500 and 27,500 to or from Griffiss Air Force Base. A few miles off to your right, the jets will be at altitudes ranging down to 6500 feet, and that's a little close. So you'll want to make certain that you are on your intended course, and it'll be a good idea to notify Griffiss that you're in the area. A quick radio conversation will let them know.

You're at the halfway point, clear of the climb corridor, on course, and making good time. Tuned back to the 73° outbound radial at Syracuse, you notice the needle slowly drifting left, toward the center of the dial. Twenty more minutes of flying time and you'll intercept that radial; at that point you'll be ten miles from Raquette Lake. The time goes quickly. The sun, off to your right, is high in the sky. The engine purrs at a steady 2350 r.p.m.'s. The omni needle is drifting a little more left. High above you, you notice a formation of jet fighters. Mountains are beginning to rise below you; you've already checked—the highest point is less than 2,000 feet above sea level, a full 2500 feet under your Cessna.

The needle is near center, a tiny bit to the right. It's

moving slowly, s-l-o-w-l-y, and it's centered. You're right on the omni radial, ten miles short of Raquette. "Coming up on Raquette Lake in exactly five minutes," you announce proudly to your passenger. It's 11:52. He smiles, checks his watch, and scratches his head in amazement at your mysterious skills.

You spot a seaplane below you, off to your left. He's getting into the traffic pattern for a landing at Raquette, and you predict aloud that he'll be turning left any moment (onto his base leg). Your passenger smiles again in wonderment, and watches the float-equipped plane make a left-hand turn. Ahead of you is Raquette. You fly over it. It's 11:57, and you're right on your estimate.

A quick call to a nearby omni station (Benson Radio, 111.8, is off to your right), and you check in: "Cessna Five Eight Seven Two Alpha, flying VFR round trip from Whit-

Cessna's Skyhawk, equipped with floats, lands on lake. Special rating is required for seaplane flying.

ford to Raquette Lake and return, over Raquette Lake at five-seven. Flying locally here for ten minutes and heading right back to Whitford."

"Roger Cessna Seven Two Alpha."

You take a longing look at the beautiful lake below, with its seaplanes. You make a slow 720° around the area, while your passenger smiles at the prospect of landing there himself someday. And you turn back to Whitford, picking up a 253° inbound radial to Syracuse Omni.

A ten-mile headwind this time. That means you'll be five minutes longer on this trip. You should arrive over Whitford at 1:12 P.M.

"What did we say?" you ask your passenger. "Did we figure we'd be back by 1:15? I estimate we'll be on the ground at exactly 1:15—let's see how close we can come. O.K.?"

PART
II

CHAPTER 7

Yaw dampers, squawk codes, and windshield heat. Those are the terms that belong in the world of the commercial airline pilot, and they are far removed from the limited horizons of the privately licensed VFR flier.

The airline pilot has a commercial license, with instrument and multiengine and air transport ratings. He is a veteran of thousands of flying hours. He is subjected to three exacting physicals a year, and he goes back to school at least twice a year for refresher courses. Typically, he knows more about emergency procedures than the VFR pilot knows about following railroad tracks to the nearest village airport. His knowledge of hydraulic systems may be greater than the whole store of knowledge that the student pilot must commit to memory. He may or may not be able to sideslip a Champ into a turf field, but he can bring a 120-ton jet to a smooth stop in a raging snowstorm, and his 130 passengers will remain as comfortable as they would in their living rooms.

The airline pilot is a walking encyclopedia of aeronautical facts. He can recite frequencies, circuitry, load factors, and a hundred other things. And he has a set of manuals at his side that will give him hundreds of thousands of other facts in a matter of moments. How good is he at looking up what he needs to know? Consider this:

The airliners are equipped with DME (distance measuring equipment), and in some cases a flight must be canceled if the DME is not working. But which cases? I asked this question of several commercial flight crews, while the airplane was flying: "Is DME a no-go item?"* It took an average of 35 seconds to get the correct answer, and in every case the men looked it up in a manual weighing more than five pounds!

The airline pilot is primarily a student. He studies flight characteristics, technical data, performance criteria, and people. He is a student of his trade, and a serious one. Changes come so fast in aviation that he can be quickly bypassed if he should decide to let up for a while.

The airline pilot is physically capable. An ailment that would force most men to "take it easy" can ground the pilot, and cost him his job: a twenty-five-year veteran can be forced to give it up overnight.**

The airline pilot is emotionally stable. There are hours of sheer boredom on long airline flights, and they sometimes are punctuated by moments of *what could be* stark terror. But a commercial cockpit is no place for a terrified man. It requires a man who knows precisely what he's doing at all times; anybody else comes off second best in a business that doesn't offer too many second chances. Terrify a planeload of passengers, including some young children and some grandmothers, and you've done incalculable harm to the airline industry. So you make your banks smooth, and your landings jolt free, and you do it every day.

The airline pilot is a quick thinker, and a man who can act quickly too. In extremely bad weather, flying solely on the instruments before him, the commercial captain is the epitome of a thinking man: The plane is several hundred feet off the ground, and descending rapidly. Outside, only

---
* It is, departing from some cities.
** Because of this, commercial pilots purchase loss-of-license insurance, which pays them up to $75,000 if a disability permanently grounds them. Regular life insurance is available at the same rate that white-collar workers pay.

a thick fog is visible. The captain's eyes zero in on several gauges, while his hands deftly maneuver the yoke and throttles.

His copilot stares out ahead, looking for the first sign of the runway. Until now, only those reliable gauges have kept them in a proper glide toward the threshold. More fog, and only the copilot's calm voice punctuates the silence.

"Three hundred feet."

More fog; the windshield looks white. The red glow of the instrument panel lights becomes the center of attention.

"Runway in sight." No raised voices here; just a calm recital of the simple fact that the airplane in which they flew 3,000 miles at nearly the speed of sound, six miles above the earth, has now come to within 250 feet of a runway.

The cockpit of a Lockheed Constellation,
used for international trips

And it's time to stop reading those gauges, and to start putting the bird on the ground.

Behind them, back in the tourist section of the huge jet, a man thumbs through his magazine. The "no-smoking" and "fasten-seat-belts" signs have been on for a few moments, and the air traveler knows it's landing time. But there are few unusual sensations. He glances at a cartoon in the magazine, and makes a mental note to tell his children about it when they meet him in the terminal in a few minutes.

Two hostesses sit side by side on a folding seat, and one complains that she ripped a stocking yesterday; they decide to go shopping together after they land.

A woman and her infant son gaze quietly out the window; they can see occasional flashes of light now through the thick fog.

"Runway in sight."

In the split moments that follow, the captain takes his eyes from the instruments and looks ahead. The runway is there, sure enough. Now he must make the transition between inanimate gauges and the real-life situation before him. Is he properly aligned? At the right altitude? Speed correct within five knots? Attitude perfect? Plenty of clear runway ahead?

Those can be the shortest seconds in a man's life. His 100-plus passengers, his aircraft, the lives of his crew and his own life depend on his split-second judgment. He hasn't seen the ground for the last thirty minutes of flight. Now—based on what he sees in the next instant—he must decide whether to land the airplane, and how.

There isn't a trace of panic, or fright. But there is a healthy respect for the realities of the situation. All the years of training are behind him, all the hours of practice a part of his memory circuit.

Inevitably, he's a little off. Quick corrections on the yoke now. A firm hand, with a soft touch, and the man and

70

machine are acting together, as planned.

Alignment perfect. Airspeed dropping off. Touchdown. Smooth. All gear firmly on the ground. Speed brakes. Reverse thrust. Brakes. The airplane becomes a ground machine, no faster than an airport truck.

They turn off onto the first taxiway, heading for the terminal.

"Flight 23 from New York arriving at Gate 9," says the voice on the loudspeaker inside.

"Ladies and gentlemen, for your own safety and comfort please remain seated until the aircraft has reached the terminal and all engines have been stopped. We are now in San Francisco, where the local time is 8:15 P.M. We remind you to check the overhead racks and the space under your seat for personal belongings. And now, on behalf of Captain Jones and the crew, we want to thank you for flying with us today, and we hope to see you aboard again soon." The sweet but professional voice of the hostess fades off, and tape-recorded music begins; the cabin is well lighted. Mother begins wrapping her infant son in a blanket against the chill air outside. The magazine is put down, the cartoon forgotten.

Ground crews begin swarming toward the jet. A signalman guides the captain into a parking job that any housewife would envy. The engines stop. The two passenger doors are opened. Hostesses stand by, flashing warm smiles.

"Good evening, sir." "By now." "Good night."

Minutes later, the flight crew leaves the airplane. The captain strides into the terminal. A man who had been his passenger spots him. "A little foggy out there, isn't it?"

"Yes, sir," replies the captain. "A little foggy."

Had it gone the other way, had the 200-foot minimum been reached with still no runway lights in sight, the same calm professionalism would have prevailed. "Minimums, no runway," the copilot would have said. And they would have added thousands of pounds of thrust to the big engines, and gone aloft again for either a later try or another airport.

Either way, it's no place for a beginner. Or for an unstable man. The training is fierce, and just one such low-visibility landing makes it all worthwhile. Even a normal landing, under ideal conditions, requires all the background a man can cram into his working lifetime.

"Landed without incident."

Those journalistic words are the goal of every airline crewman. Everything that's done is in that direction. A flight without complications. You'll read about the one tire that blows out, but you won't read about the thousands of flights every day that are made without incident. Or the tens of thousands of people who make them happen that way.

A single major air carrier is an organized morass of activity-bound people. Trans World Airlines, the system I spent months working with to get the information for this book, is a web of efficiency spreading around the world. Let one flight be late—for any reason—and TWA headquarters knows about it, and is asking why. Radio trouble on a flight from Cleveland to Chicago, and maintenance people are asking questions. Ramp scheduling difficulties at John F. Kennedy Airport in New York, and other people are working to untangle the maze. A balky altimeter in Los Angeles, and experts are figuring out the answers. A rough engine in St. Louis; a damaged turbine in Denver; a severe weather front in Pittsburgh—what happened, and why, and how can we help?

The nerve center for all TWA flight operations is located in Kansas City.

Gathered there every morning at 8:45 are key executives, department and division heads, for a review and summary of the past twenty-four hours of operation. The review covers every damage to an aircraft, every return from

*Vital information is shared during daily
morning briefings at TWA base in Kansas City.*

flight, every aborted takeoff, every return from runway, and
every major mechanical delay.

The airline operates hundreds of flights a day in the
United States alone. On each landing, the crew is met by
a maintenance man to discuss the condition of the aircraft.
If a malfunction exists, it's corrected before the flight continues.

In addition to that, each plane gets a periodic checkup
and regularly scheduled overhauls. Everything gets looked
at: one of Kansas City's jobs is to pronounce airplanes fit
for action, and they don't get the stamp until they've been
exposed to everything from engine testing to X-rays.

Some of the problems are more annoying than dangerous.
Carpeting, for example. The planes are carpeted throughout, but naturally take more wear near the doors and in
front of each seat. But carpeting under the seats takes no
wear at all. For years, the airline was throwing away huge
strips of beautiful carpet—alternately brand-new and worn,
brand-new and worn, every couple of feet. Then an em-

ployee had a bright idea: why not pull the whole strip of carpet back a couple of feet, adding one small piece at the end? That way, the section under a seat (virtually unscathed) would become the section in front of the seat behind. He won a substantial prize for his idea, which later became standard airline procedure.

But the major thought at Kansas City is safety, and the byword is "test." Everything gets tested; instruments are overhauled, engines rebuilt, landing gear restructured. And then it's all subjected to a series of exhaustive tests. An airplane coming out of Kansas City's $25 million overhaul base is as good as new—better, now that some earlier bugs have been taken out of it.

But safety starts long before that. First, thorough service checks are made without fail every day, according to a booklet TWA has begun distributing to its passengers.

A huge jet undergoes overhauling in work dock.

Every 130 hours of flight time, piston aircraft receive the general station service check. Every 500 hours an infinitely more comprehensive maintenance check is performed, in which every part is thoroughly examined.

Every 1900 to 2500 hours, piston engines are disassembled and replaced with other completely overhauled engines. (Jet engines can go up to 4600 hours between overhauls.) Approximately midway through overhaul time, jet engines are partially disassembled for inspection and replacement of critical parts. Engines are periodically changed, whether they show wear or not, whenever they no longer deliver the required maximum horsepower or thrust.

Last comes the big check, the base overhaul for jets, every 6,000 hours. This major inspection of the entire aircraft leaves it literally better than it was new. A TWA plane is first washed down from head to foot with 300 gallons of solvents. Seats, carpets, and galleys are taken out for cleaning or replacement. Instruments are removed, overhauled, and precisely checked for accuracy. Electrical wiring—the jet's entire 40 miles of it—is thoroughly checked. Tires, wheels, and brakes get the twice-over.

It takes fifteen workdays (2300 man-hours) to overhaul a jet engine. And the cost for four of them runs as high as $120,000.

Each part is sent through a series of soak tanks in which those parts bearing carbon deposits are blasted with millions of tiny glass beads. Each part is X-rayed for cracks and wear. Rotor and turbine blades by the hundreds are separated from their supports, cleaned, inspected for nicks, and replaced if necessary by spare parts of precisely the same weight.

When reassembled, the engine is placed in a test cell and tested by an engineer whose instruments explore its innermost secrets—recording each one. One tiny flaw, and back it goes for more service. During these tests, an engine generally consumes 1800 gallons of fuel—enough for a good-sized Convair 880 trip.

If you were to apply the same system to your car, the TWA booklet advises, you would inspect it visually every time you drove it, replace all five tires every 750 miles, overhaul the engine every 20,000 miles, and reupholster and repaint it every 50,000 miles.

At each terminal, too, people are just as worried about that single goal, transporting people safely. A jet taxis in, and people go into action. Before the flight crew has finished its checkout procedures, the ground crewmen are busy. Somebody has to get steps up to the airplane doors. Somebody has to point the way into the terminal for the line of passengers debarking. Other somebodies have to get the airplane nourished for another flight.

I spent a whole day watching TWA ground crews operate at an East Coast airport. Three men handled fuel and water (for the water-injection models of the Boeing 707 jet). Five men worked getting baggage off the airplane, and new baggage loaded. One man handled the commissary supplies. Two men cleaned the cabin. Three transportation agents were busy with passengers' details. There were nineteen people working on that one flight. They loaded 2,000 gallons of fuel and 371 gallons of demineralized water (processed right at the airport). They supervised the stacking of more than a hundred meals. They made certain that film was on board for in-flight movies. They checked everything from carpeting to coffee, from tires to tea bags. And they did it so quickly that it would have required three men to watch without missing anything.

It takes 150 ground people at that one station to service some twenty flights a day.

They put the airplane in ready condition. And then the flight crew takes over. Hostesses buzz about the cabin, checking needed supplies. The flight engineer makes an exhaustive preflight check. The first officer (copilot) files a flight plan, and checks enroute weather, radio frequencies, traffic routing, and myriad other details. The captain, responsible for it all, double-checks everybody else. It is he who must accept or reject the planned route and its details. He must be satisfied with his flight engineer's assurances, and with his first officer's calculations. He knows exactly how many people are on board, how much the fuel weighs, how fast the airplane will have to be moving before it will lift off. He knows where they'll go if weather intervenes at the other end of their trip. He knows how much fuel they'll have to turn getting there, or to a second alternate field.

And when the flight is over, it is the captain who will rate the performance of his crew.

How good are they? Strip the glamour from those men, and rate them objectively. Take away the mysterious aura surrounding them, and take a close, impersonal look at their efficiency. How good are they?

Very good.

On a short jet hop into Pittsburgh, I listened on earphones as a first officer took down instructions from air traffic control. "Maintain four thousand," the voice said in a welter of static. "Did he say four?" asked the captain. The first officer, without bothering to recheck his own penciled notation, said, "No. Seven, wasn't it?"

"No. Four," replied the captain.

The first officer rechecked. "You're right," he said.

I didn't see the man's performance rating, but I'd be willing to bet that his captain wasn't satisfied. No harm done. It was an almost insignificant thing; they were climbing out, and had reached only 2,000 feet. The first officer had it down on paper, and he had it correct. But his momentary lapse isn't supposed to happen, and the captain's raised eyebrow would be transformed into a marking later on that would be less than perfect. The first officer wasn't a captain yet.

A few moments later, on that same flight, radar control

informed the crew that there was traffic ten miles ahead. "Dead ahead," said the captain, in an instant. "See him?"

"Got him," said the first officer. There was no danger involved. It was merely a routine warning to the crews of both planes that the other was in the vicinity. Radar had them both spotted, and was letting them know about it. But the captain, busy flying the airplane and concerned with the performance of his entire crew (plus the accuracy of this flight), was the man who spotted the other airplane.

On another flight, the captain was making an intricate approach into busy Kennedy Airport in New York. He was less than a thousand feet from the ground when a rookie hostess rang him on the intercom. "Excuse me," she said, "but I have a man back here who has to make a 12:37 connection. Can he make it?"

"Well, since it's 12:42 now, I doubt it," said the captain, returning to the job at hand.

The rather curt reply to the needless question may have bothered the hostess, but the point is that the interruption didn't bother the captain.

How good?

Very good.

CHAPTER 8

The men who fly the big jets are professionals, but they are men. The pilot's biggest job is to subdue the manlike frailties, and let professionalism rule. At any given point in a flight, he may suddenly have to recall a fact or a regulation learned years ago, and immediately put it into practice. Only the pro can be called upon to do it, day after day, and do it right.

Sometimes it doesn't work that way. Airline pilots are fond of telling about the copilot who flew a certain model piston-engine plane for eight years, then transferred over to a new model. When the captain asked him to close the cowl flaps, he reached over for the handle he had reached for thousands of times in the past. But the new model was different, and what he pulled was the landing gear lever. The gear retracted, and the big airplane plopped down quite unladylike—right there outside the terminal building.

The story may not be true, but its sequel is. Landing gear levers in airplanes today are shaped like landing gear, complete with a little wheel. Not even the greenest pilot can miss it.

The moral? Every mistake seems to produce another change in the airlines business. Changes come by the thousands, every year. Equipment changes and keeps getting better (and incidentally, trickier to operate). And the regulations change. Pilots have more to do. They have more

79

procedures to follow. And more to learn.

Somebody once erred while leveling off at a specified altitude. The pilots weren't watching carefully enough, and they got higher than they were supposed to. Serious accidents can happen that way. So now there's a regulation which says that the copilot must notify the pilot one thousand feet before they reach the target altitude. "Leaving thirty-two (thousand feet) for thirty-three," the first officer says, and nobody makes that particular kind of mistake anymore.

Air traffic control centers give clearances by the thousands too. Back in the dim past, pilots would occasionally misunderstand a clearance, or vital parts of landing instructions. Today the pilot is required to repeat it, so that the center can verify its own instructions.

All along the line, the pilots are working harder than ever before, doing more things, keeping track of more details. And the more they do, the more important it becomes that they have good crews working with them.

Basically, the first officer's job is to assist the captain with the paper work and the radio work of a flight. The flight engineer is concerned with the mechanical performance of the airplane—its pressurization system, fuel consumption, and engines.

The details begin long before the flight leaves the ground. Take a typical trip, TWA Flight 181 out of Philadelphia, bound for O'Hare International Airport in Chicago on a hot July evening. Its departure time is 10:10. Before 9, its flight crew shows up to go to work.

The captain is twenty-year veteran Lyle Ryan of Chicago, who had 3500 hours of wartime Air Force service before he began flying DC-3's for TWA in 1945. Later he flew the Boeing Stratoliner, the DC-4, and the Constellation. Then he switched over to Convair 880 jets. Back in 1945, he was working for a starting salary of $220 a month ("I took quite a pay cut to get the job," he says). But today he averages

The Boeing 707 Star Stream ↑

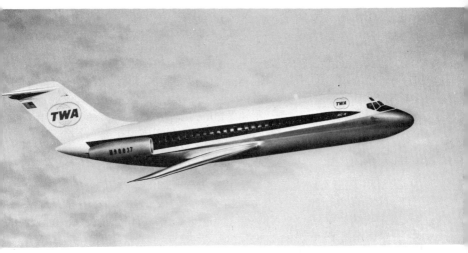

Douglas Aircraft's short-haul DC–9 ↑   *The Convair 880 Superjet* ↓

ten times as much and more, flying his required eighty hours a month on TWA's domestic routes.

The first officer is 28-year-old Greg Gollnick, who learned to fly in the Navy and acquired 1500 hours of flying time in pistons and jets. He went to work for Trans World on January 13, 1964; he earned $500 a month as a student. He spent six weeks in second officers school, spent eight months flying on the line, and then went back to school to become a first officer (copilot) on the Connies, the famous Constellations that TWA was phasing out while planning for an all-jet fleet. It was back on the line for seven months, and then back to school again, this time to learn first officer's duties on the 880 jet. Today Greg averages $850 to $900 a month in take-home pay.

Ryan, Gollnick, and flight engineer Ralph Jones had been flying together as a crew for more than fifteen hours over the past two days before they made this Philadelphia-Chicago trip. They had gone to Albuquerque and Tucson, spent the night in Phoenix, gone on to Los Angeles and San Francisco, then left Los Angeles for Phoenix, Tucson, Albuquerque, Chicago, and Philadelphia. Now they were one short trip away from going home. They had been away for fifty-eight hours, and will have logged sixteen hours of flying time when the trip is over.

The 880 they are flying tonight seats 22 first-class passengers and 72 tourist-class ones. They have four hostesses, the Misses Friedley, Moyer, Coatney, and Loer, assigned to the flight.

There is no weather problem tonight, but there is a lot of haze over the East Coast. On the trip in, they flew at 25,000 feet and had a smooth ride. They'd heard that planes flying a lot higher had experienced a good deal of choppy weather, and so Captain Ryan had decided to request a clearance of 26,000 feet on the way back home.

Flight 181 is scheduled to leave Philadelphia at 10:10 P.M. and arrive at O'Hare at 10:59 C.S.T.—an hour and forty-nine minutes from gate to gate (block time). Greg Gollnick's manuals tell him that they will leave Philadelphia via a *Lancaster One* departure, leaving on Runway 27 and flying that heading until they reach an altitude of 2,000 feet. Then they'll make a right turn to a heading of 350 degrees and head for their assigned jet airway. They'll fly to checkpoints with the names Pittsburgh and Allegheny, and head into Chicago.

Gollnick is hard at work, filling out a flight log form, predicting flying times and fuel consumption, and a dozen other things. He knows that the FAA requires reserve fuel of 5500 pounds on this trip, and that TWA requires another 2500 beyond that. He determines his planned altitude (26,000 feet), his average temperature ($-26°$ centigrade), and computes his true airspeed figure for the trip—503 knots. Figuring in a headwind, he determines that the speed will actually be 443 knots. Based on that information, and adding things like the actual ground miles covered, he can compute the total fuel they'll use getting into Chicago—a total of 24,000 pounds.

New York has advised that this trip can leave with 40,000 pounds of fuel, which means that they'll have a total of 16,000 pounds in reserve when they leave Philadelphia International.

Gollnick inserts other vital information: the OWE (operating weight empty) for the Convair 880 is 89,400 pounds. His estimated pay load is 12,000 pounds, and figuring in his fuel, his takeoff weight should be 141,400 pounds. Subtracting the fuel they'll burn tonight, he gets his landing weight, 117,400 pounds.

Every figure is important. The jets operate at close tolerances, and items like takeoff, landing, and approach speeds are carefully calculated after those initial figures are determined. Back in the Cessna, Greg Gollnick could have landed at less than 60 m.p.h. Tonight they'll be going into O'Hare at twice that speed and more, and a 10-knot miscalculation could endanger the whole flight.

Gollnick is back into the charts, determining that at a gross weight of 145,000 pounds, aiming at 26,000 feet and in −26° centigrade temperature, it will take them 16 minutes to climb to their altitude. During that time they will have covered 103 miles over the ground and burned 6,210 pounds of fuel, at an average true airspeed of 444 knots. His calculations show him that the whole flight should take an hour and thirty-three minutes; the book says it will take them 1:36, and Gollnick splits the difference and estimates 1:34.

At 79° F. outside temperature, with an altimeter (barometric pressure) setting of 29.93, the book says they can leave with the maximum gross weight tonight—184,500 pounds. Their planned weight of 141,400 is well below that.

Next, Gollnick calculates a particularly vital speed, called V_1. It is at V_1 (which for this flight will be 147 knots) that Flight 181 will be committed to a takeoff. After reaching V_1, there won't be enough runway left to abort the takeoff. No matter what happens, they'll be heading for takeoff after this plane gets up to 147 knots tonight.

There are other key speeds as well. One is V_r—the speed at which they can rotate (lift off). And there is V_2—the speed at which the big jet will fly. And V_{mca}—the plane's minimum controllable airspeed.

Normally, V_r, V_2, and V_{mca} would be considerably higher than the V_1 speed. But tonight, based on pay load, fuel load, temperature, runway length, and barometric pressure, that V_1 speed will be reached when the plane is safely airborne. V_{mca} is relatively slow for this trip. There will be plenty of runway. Gollnick will determine the V_r and V_2 speeds when he gets a weight-balance sheet from the ground agent before they leave the gate. (It is that weight-balance sheet that you see being handed up on a long pole to the pilot after the airliner's engines are started, and before he begins to taxi.)

Tonight's weight-balance sheet shows that the front cargo

84

compartment carries 3,781 pounds, and the rear compartment 2,896. There had been reservations for 10 first-class passengers, and 38 tourist, but last-minute customers brought that total up to 11 first and 47 tourist. The ground agent figures that each passenger weighs 165 pounds average.*

Flight 181's actual gross takeoff weight tonight will be 144,025 pounds. Based on that, Gollnick quickly figures that V_2 speed will be 145 knots—the same as their minimum controllable airspeed. Their V_r speed will be 15 knots slower—130.

At 10:10 P.M. (schedules are taken seriously), TWA Flight 181 starts from the gate for Runway 27. Exactly six minutes later, it is airborne.

(Gollnick had estimated 1:34 flying time, but they will encounter very little traffic going into the landing pattern at O'Hare, and their time will be cut to 1:30. He had figured 1:49 block time; they will make it tonight in 1:42, arriving at 10:52 Chicago time.)

Captain Ryan has high praise for Greg Gollnick. "He's got the right attitude, and he's plenty smooth," Ryan says. "He'll make a good airline pilot. He's good on the paper work too."

Gollnick has to be. His job includes looking up V-speeds, weights, and air routes for every flight. And every flight is different. Ryan, the veteran of two decades in the air for his company, is responsible for it. But young Greg Gollnick bears the brunt of the paper work every time he flies.

Chances are that Ryan and Gollnick won't be flying together for a year after tonight. Their schedules will take them different ways, to different parts of the country, on different airplanes. When they next meet, Gollnick will have nearly another thousand hours' flying time. He will

* In summertime. In winter, the average passenger weight is figured at 170 pounds to allow for heavier clothing.

have made many takeoffs and landings in the 880 during that time, under the close supervision of the pilot sitting to his left.

And he will have turned tens of thousands of pages in his books, looking up flight data.

"It's exactly what I want to be doing," he says. "I love it."

And that's precisely what Captain Lyle Ryan means by attitude. "What do you look for first in a green copilot?" I asked him. "Attitude," he replied. "Does the man love his job? Does he really *want* to fly? Enough to work hard at it?" In Ryan's estimation, Gollnick rated high on attitude.

I asked the same question of Charles O. Church, TWA's chief (domestic routes) pilot in New York. And he gave the same reply. "I guess you'd have to say that attitude is most important," he said. "Sure, the man must be able to handle the radio job, and all the paper work. But even if he makes small mistakes, we can overlook them. After all, that's what we have an experienced captain sitting there for—to make sure that an inexperienced man's mistakes don't hurt anybody.

"We'll forgive mistakes, but we aren't so tolerant when it comes to attitude. We want to hire men who will be wanting to do their jobs. This is a job that requires a very special kind of man. There is a heavy load of detail, and it never lets up. There are different captains to fly with. In the old days, one captain would fly with one copilot for a long period of time. Now our schedules don't permit that kind of inflexibility. We need first officers who will get along with their captains—who will recognize that their primary job is to assist the captain. And for that, you need the right kind of attitude."

Another captain told me, "I want to make certain that the man is neat, clean, and on time. You can gauge his attitude from things like that. If he's late, he's going to be late doing other things as well. And we can't afford to take tardiness lightly in this business; things happen too fast too often. If he's not neat, he is demonstrating that he doesn't really *care*. And if he doesn't care about himself, how can he be expected to care about a $6 million airplane, and a hundred people on board?"

In several months of flying with TWA crews, I never met a man who wasn't neat, clean, and on time. Now I know why.

CHAPTER 9

TWA flight crews get their training at a school that specializes in details. The details are as realistic as TWA can make them.

I sat in the cockpit of a 707 jet, watching a young pilot cope with one of aviation's worst hazards—fire. We had just taken off, and the runway disappeared from view underneath us, when suddenly lights and bells began going off in the cockpit. The pilot began reacting immediately. In an effort to determine the exact cause of the fire, he started taking precisely prescribed remedial steps:

> Throttle closed; essential power check; yaw damper off; nacelle anti-ice off; start lever off; fire control pulled; fire extinguisher discharged; electrical power checked; pressurization system checked; and other steps taken to assure that the airplane is still flyable. (The last step: "If fire persists, proceed to the nearest landing facility.")

But the fire was out. The instructor sitting beside him said simply, "Good. Now let's try a two-engine missed approach." And they started again. Emergency after emergency cropped up, while the instructor evaluated his student's ability to cope with them calmly and correctly. Engines suddenly lost power; near stalls occurred at unexpected intervals; pressurization failed suddenly. At each crisis, the student in the cockpit was expected to take firm corrective action in one-two-three order, with no delays. He had to know his procedures in advance.

When the session was over, the student was smiling but perspiring heavily. "He's had more emergencies today than he'd get in a decade of flying," the instructor said.

The two of them stepped out of the cockpit—and into a large, well-lighted room on the eighth floor of a building in downtown Kansas City.

The cockpit was real enough; every switch, control, and gauge worked. But the whole thing is a complex $1 million simulator, firmly rooted to the floor of the building. Sitting in the captain's seat, actuating the controls for a takeoff, the student sees the runway ahead of him and hears the engines pick up speed. As he reaches rotating speed and

Simulator of the Boeing 707 model 131
with water-injection system for takeoffs

starts to lift off, the runway drops from sight. On landings, he can see the plane coming down onto the strip, feel the bump when contact is made, and hear the screech of the tires on impact. Even turbulence is duplicated: the cockpit bounces around in response to programmed choppy air.

It's a safe, inexpensive way of drilling emergency procedures into students. Boeing 707's cost maybe $1,000 an hour to fly; the simulator can be "flown" at one fifth the cost, and at no danger to the airplane or its crew. The 707 and Convair 880 simulators log about 15,000 hours of in-use time a year.

A closed-circuit television system provides the realistic views from the cockpit. In an adjoining room, perched on its side, is a real-enough-looking runway, complete with bordering trees, vehicles, and buildings. A TV camera

By turning photo on left side, TWA's model
"runway on a wall" looks like the real thing.

Cockpit view shows landing in simulator at Kansas City, heading toward projected TV view on screen ahead.

mounted on its side begins its travel at the beginning of the runway, and moves down it at appropriate speed as the simulator controls are actuated by the student. What the student sees is the runway picture projected onto a screen mounted in front of the cockpit.

How realistic is it? I felt I'd been flying when I left the cockpit, and so do the students. The cockpit door is closed; everything looks the same, sounds the same, smells the same, and feels the same as in an airplane aloft. "Sure is a strange feeling," muttered one student after his first "ride" in the simulator.

Another innovation is the animated training boards used to depict graphically the workings of jet systems. One out-

lines in lights and brightly colored lines the landing gear
system of the 707. Pull the lever and a wheel descends into
position, activating lights like those found on the 707 control panel.

Other training boards depict the innards of electrical,
navigation, anti-ice, hydraulic brakes, flight director, and air
conditioning systems, and of such other workings as flap
operations.

*The Convair 880 simulator. Note darkened
screen ahead of plane.*

An animated cutaway version of a jet engine, encased in
glass, shows exactly how the powerful engine works. Instruments above the engine show static air temperature, ram air
temperature, r.p.m.'s, fuel flow, pressure ratio, burner pres-

*Cutaway views help pilots understand
jet engine operation.*

sure, exhaust temperature, airspeed, and altitude.

Films, sound tapes, visual aids, and projection equipment round out the training devices. The byword is realism; the goal is a thorough grasp of the airplane's workings, and no student can avoid it. Even hallway wall space is used: little boxes contain a list of questions and rows of buttons. Pick a flight problem while you're waiting for an elevator, press a button, and the board tells you if your answer is correct.

The training school produces cardboard-mounted photos of flight panels, which the student can tack to the wall over his bed.

And, of course, there are training manuals. Manuals cover every phase of pilotage, from navigation to emergency procedures.

Students (maybe 7500 or more a year)* spend weeks of intensified training at the school, which is so popular it attracts pilots from other airlines and also the pilots who fly the President's jets.

But the real training—as the school admits—comes

* The school also trains flight engineers, hostesses, and ground personnel.

93

through experience on the line. It is in the real cockpit, facing real situations, that the pilot learns by actually doing. The school, simulators and all, can only be a prelude to actual line operations. The same words heard by the newly licensed private pilot are heard by new graduates at the school: "Now you can really start to learn."

In the cockpit, training is up to the captain. It is he who authorizes the copilot to make takeoffs and landings, or fly headings, or change altitudes. It is he who supervises every inch of line training the young first officer gets. Beyond that, the copilot can help himself by thinking through everything the captain does, and by absorbing everything in sight.

"I'm a student up there, and I'll be a student for a long time," a first officer told me. "Come to think of it, I don't think I'll ever stop being a student. At least I hope I never stop being one. There's too much to learn in this trade." That kind of attitude is what pilots Church, Kadoch, and others had in mind when they talked about young pilots.

What, exactly, *does* the young pilot have to learn? Here is a partial list for a 707 pilot:

Mechanical workings of the aircraft—air frame and power plant and all its systems; every flight emergency procedure ever devised, for any kind of crisis from fire to fog; a thorough knowledge of civil air regulations; navigation systems and techniques; a complete understanding of jet airways, departures, and approaches under any climatic conditions; a complete understanding of weather and its effects on flying; a good understanding of aerodynamics, and a complete understanding of the airplane's flying characteristics; good radio procedures; company rules, regulations, and policies; a working knowledge of the company and its many facets of operation, such as line maintenance and scheduling; a good understanding of customer and public relations, and on, and on, and on . . .

For the pilot making the piston-to-jet transition, there are other vital fundamentals. The jet handles differently. Speeds and techniques are more critical. You can get into trouble more quickly, if you don't know what you're doing.

One example: stalling a light plane can be easy, and even fun. A good recovery technique can be learned in a matter of minutes, and a little practice is all that's needed for pilot mastery. Stalling a piston-engine airliner is more complicated; the stalls come easier and faster and with less warning. But stalling a jet can be the trickiest of all. In some situations, cruise speed and stalling speed may be just 30 k. apart. (Normal variation: 70 knots.) It is true that the jet has its warnings (including an automatic stick vibrator). It rumbles and shudders slightly before breaking into the stall itself. If you catch it at the first rumble, say the veteran pilots, you can recover within 300 to 500 feet. But let it get past that first sign of aerodynamic instability, and the plane will plunge *thousands of feet* before you can recover. It's happened, too. Several airline pilots learned about it the hard way, encountering severe turbulence in clear air. If they hadn't demonstrated superior airmanship, they wouldn't be alive to tell about it, and we would know a good deal less about turbulence and its effects, and how to deal with it.

The jets, unlike the pistons, have swept wings—with entirely different aerodynamic properties. They have far more power, which means a different kind of handling. They need more speed for takeoff. They land faster. All of this has to be experienced. The student jet pilot learns about the jet's theoretical operation in the classroom, and from books. He learns how it handles from sitting in simulators. He learns more by flying it.

Actual flights are made by students, who must demonstrate such techniques as stall recoveries. Veteran instructors sit at their sides, inserting new problems into the well-planned flight. Engines are throttled back, unusual flight attitudes are encountered, and it's something like learning to fly over again. The student who comes out of it is the

95

best-trained student that the airline can produce. He is a budding jet pilot. He may be green, but he's got more practical knowledge than he's ever had. Or, for that matter, than any young airline pilot in history has ever had.

All together, the jet pilot training curriculum contains thirty-four hours of basic course material, and sixty-nine hours in the qualification course for either the Boeing or the Convair jets. The basic course covers introduction and orientation (30 minutes); general aircraft study (1:30); performance, meteorology, and flight planning (12:00); power plant—fuel, oil, fire control, and nacelle anti-ice (3:00); hydraulic, flight, and small systems (1:30); instruments and electronics (6:00); electrical system (1:30); air conditioning, pressurization, anti-ice, and bleed air (1:30); physiology (1:30); classroom, cabin-trainer drills and jet regulations (2:00); films (1:30); and an examination (1:30). The qualification course also includes an hour and a half on flight techniques, and three hours on emergency equipment, evacuation, and ditching procedures. In addition, it includes many more detailed hours spent in the study of power plant and airplane systems.

Landing one of the big jets can be complicated. First, it depends on what kind of approach is made. TWA specifies several. In a normal landing, the airplane is 1500 feet off the ground as it flies through the landing pattern. Ten to fifteen minutes before arrival, the flight crew has gone through a preliminary checklist. At a predetermined point in the pattern, flaps are lowered to a specified position, and minimum airspeed must be V_{ref} (which is 1.3 stalling speed) plus 30 knots. Halfway down the downwind leg, minimum speed is reduced to V_{ref} plus 20 knots. Just before turning base, landing gear is lowered.

As the base leg is turned, flaps are lowered to 40 degrees, and speed reduced to V_{ref} plus 10 knots, and a normal descent is begun.

As the pilot turns onto final, at 500 to 800 feet, he increases flaps to a 50-degree setting, and reduces speed to V_{ref} plus 5 knots. He aims to touch down 1,000 feet from the threshold of the runway.

The pilot and first officer have a seven-point checklist that must be completed just before landing, and another eight points to check right after completing the landing roll. Put the verbal checklist and the verbal landing orders together, and the cockpit becomes a conversational hotbox on landing. The checklist alone sounds something like this:

Second officer: "Landing gear."

Captain: "Down and three green lights."

Second officer: "Yaw damper."

Captain: "Check."

Second officer: "No-smoking sign."

Captain: "On."

Second officer: "Anti-skid."

Captain: "On and four releases."

Second officer: "Altimeters."

Captain: "Set and cross-check."

Second officer: "Rudder auxiliary pump."

Captain: "On."

Second officer: "Rudder and hydraulic system pressure."

Captain: "Check."

(While this is going on, the flight engineer has his own checklist questions to answer.)

There are several rules of thumb for maneuvering speed and gust speed. Minimum maneuvering speed requires that the pilot add one knot to V_{ref} for each degree of flap less than 50°, and the book says that "this will provide a safe maneuvering speed up to 38° of bank. If the wind is over 20 knots with gusts, the pilot adds 5 knots to his airspeed, plus half the gust factor. Thus, if the wind is 20 with gusts up to 30, he would add 5, plus another 5 for the gust factor.

(And there is also a missed-approach procedure: "Apply takeoff thrust and rotate to climb attitude; retract flaps to 30°; positive rate of climb—up gear; maintain V_{ref} to V_{ref}

+ 5 knots. If V_{ref} is below 130 knots, slowly accelerate to 130 knots; maximum body angle 15°; at minimum of 800 feet while accelerating, V_{ref} + 10 knots, flaps 20°.")

That's a normal landing in a Boeing 707 jet (of which there are six distinct models, requiring different flap settings).

On an instrument approach, things change radically. Initially, flaps are set at 40°, gear is down, and speed is V_{ref} + 10 knots. The downwind leg is a mile and a half from the runway. Minimum altitude turning base is 500 feet. When the descent is started, flaps are at 50° and speed is V_{ref} plus 5 knots. Normally, the bank angle is less than 30°.

Another procedure is for precision approach radar (PAR). The approach to the runway is made on what appears to be an extremely long base leg. At a specified point, the pilot makes a "procedure turn." Just before he does, flaps have been increased from 20° to 30°, and speed decreased from V_{ref} + 30 k. to V_{ref} + 20 k. On final approach, flaps go to 40° and speed down to V_{ref} + 10 k. There is a straight-in approach procedure too.

There are also specified flap settings and speeds for omni, localizer, automatic direction finder, and aircraft surveillance radar procedures, for two-engine enroute climbs, missed approaches(three or four engines) from landing configurations, and something called a "canyon approach."*

Those are the landing procedures. There are takeoff procedures as well, including one which specifies what must be done when an engine fails after V_1 speed is reached on the runway.

The budding pilot learns them all.

And there is still more. The instruments on jets are much more sophisticated than ones on light planes, and so are the modern navigation systems used.

---

* It was put in the books to allow for landings between high mountains, but veteran TWA pilots who have flown all over the world confessed to me that they'd never used it.

First there is all-weather radar. Special radar with an adjustable scope detects cloud formations and other bad weather conditions up to 150 miles ahead along the route, and about 150 miles to either side. The pilot, with air route traffic control clearance, can alter course, climb or descend —for the customer's maximum comfort.

The *Instrument Landing System* (ILS) works something like this: As the aircraft approaches the airport, with the way clear for it to land, it descends to an altitude of approximately 1200 feet, makes an approach run, and turns into final. In doing so, it picks up two radio beams being transmitted by the ILS unit on the ground. Transmitted upward from the runway at a 3-degree angle, the beams form an invisible glide path and activate an indicator with two needles on the instrument panel. One beam influences a needle that shows the left and right limits (deviation) of the approach path; the other actuates a needle that shows the proper rate of descent for approach and landing (glide scope).

To make a perfect approach and landing, the pilot— watching the two proper instruments—must keep the two needles centered.

Near the ILS instrument in the cockpit are two lights, one purple and the other amber. When the purple light flashes, the pilot knows he has passed through a vertical radio beacon called the outer marker, which is located a fixed distance from the end of the runway. Seconds later, the amber light blinks on, indicating that the plane has passed through a second beacon, the inner marker, located a specified distance from the end of the runway. Since the pilot can now see a string of approach lights directly to the strip, the landing becomes visual.

Speed Command-Altitude/Target (SCAT) is an angle-accelerometer computer that helps the pilot maintain precise airspeed control during takeoff and approach to landing. SCAT senses any speed change, even before the change can register on the plane's airspeed indicator, and relays the information to a "Slow-on-speed-fast" meter. Thus the pilot is able to anticipate speed changes, and make corrections ahead of time. SCAT installation also tells the pilot how to position the airplane for climb-out by computed reference on the artificial horizon.

The *Doppler Navigation System*, the most advanced and precise method of navigation so far developed, was pioneered by TWA and introduced on the company's transatlantic flights in 1962.

The Doppler system, which employs a highly specialized form of radar, is a wholly self-contained navigation unit operated by the captain or first officer. It requires no ground aids. Radar signals from the plane are reflected from the earth's surface, either land or water, back to the plane's computer circuits, connected to indicators on the instrument panel. These indicators give the pilot instantaneous and continuous readings of ground speed, miles to go to destination, and the angle at which the plane might be drifting due to crosswinds.

The initial Doppler navigation flight across the Atlantic was the first time celestial navigation was not used on an ocean crossing. Formerly, the navigator would use a periscopic sextant—highly refined, automatic, and far more accurate than marine versions—to take observations of stars for determining the aircraft's "fix."

Since three observations per fix, plus calculations and plotting on a chart all take about fifteen minutes, a 600-m.p.h. jet would be 150 miles beyond the sextant position by the time the fix was plotted. The Doppler system tells the pilot what the aircraft is doing at any given moment.

There are also automatic direction finders, distance measuring equipment, and that old private pilot's standby— omni.

Among them, the twentieth-century jet pilot has a good chance of finding his way around the skies.

CHAPTER 10

The typical TWA captain may be personified in a huge, effervescent man whose first experience with airplanes almost convinced him never to fly.

In the early 1930's, young towheaded Bob Kadoch (pronounced KAY-dock) hitched a ride to a small airport in Aurora, Illinois, with $5 in his pocket and a burning ambition to get an airplane ride. He'd heard that a pilot was giving rides in old World War I Jennys. He arrived at the field in time to see the pilot crash a Jenny on its nose, and walk out unscathed.

The angry young pilot, with more misguided courage than experience, went over to the other side of the field and got

Charles and Palmer Church, father and son, with
Pilot Bob Kadoch, who taught the elder Church to fly

into a second Jenny. Within minutes he'd put that one on its nose too, and was dead.

Bob Kadoch walked away with a good deal of fear and an indelible respect for airplanes.

Today, more than a quarter century later, Robert A. Kadoch still has a healthy respect for airplanes. Today they are 707 jets, which he flies for a living.

It took several years after that to get the young Kadoch into flying. He finally soloed an airplane (not a Jenny) in 1936; his teacher was John Harrington, now a TWA vice-president. "I'd had about ten hours of instruction, almost all of it in takeoffs and landings," he says. "And I don't think I'll ever forget that initial thrill."

After solo, Bob and several friends pooled their money for gasoline, did odd jobs around the little airport in East St. Louis, and earned their private licenses. Flying was fast becoming a wealthy man's hobby in those days, and Bob logged many hours by ferrying airplanes (he paid for the gas) to their new owners. In 1940 he qualified for a commercial license and was offered his first full-time flying job. It paid $15 a week for stunting and charter work, and he would have had to sleep in a hangar. He turned it down.

Instead, he did some more ferrying, and some passenger-carrying, and some instruction. One of his students (in a Piper J-3 Cub) was Charles O. Church, who later became TWA's chief domestic routes pilot in New York.

Some of Bob's early flying jobs didn't work out too well. On one occasion, Bob and another pilot were hired by a local florist to drop a thousand roses on a fashionable garden party. Bob held the roses loose on his lap. When he stood up in the open cockpit to get a better view of the target zone, the roses caught in the slipstream and flew back at his face—and on out into the air. "I had thorns in me for the better part of a day," he says.

On July 18, 1941, Bob Kadoch went to work for Trans World Airlines, flying DC-2's and later DC-3's. In 1942, still as a copilot, he was sent to Alaska to haul wartime freight to the Aleutians.

Airline pilots were subject to immediate call by the Government in those days. Kadoch received his call soon after he checked out as a captain in April, 1943. He was sent to Florida to train crews who soon would be flying C-46's over the hump in the China-Burma-India theater. The crews were given two-week sessions in which to train pilot, copilot, crew chief, and navigator for the historic assignments.

By January, 1944, he was back on the line, still flying the DC-3's. Later it was the Boeing Stratoliner, and then the Constellations. By 1959 he had 17,000 hours in piston-engine aircraft.

Late in 1959, with everything completed at Boeing 707 school, he was ready to take his last check flight. But Kansas City was struck by a lengthy spell of particularly bad weather, and Bob made thirteen dry runs from his hotel to the Mid-Continent International Airport there, trying to get the check-ride. It—and his qualification—came in January, 1960.

Bob flew domestic routes, then went on TWA's international circuit, and subsequently went back to the states again, flying almost every model of the 707 from the water-injection 131 ("The Water Wagon") to the fan-engine intercontinental 331-B.

While I was working with Bob Kadoch for the background on this book, he celebrated his twenty-fourth year with TWA. In all that time, plus the time that he put in airplanes before going with the company, he'd had one close call.

It came on the East Coast, during the hunting season, when pheasants buzzed the airport regularly. His copilot was making the takeoff, and they had just reached V_1 (the speed at which they were committed to leave the ground). At that moment, he saw two pheasants flying down the runway toward the left side of their airplane. One went on by, but the other one was sucked up into the number one engine.

The engine suffered a compression stall; not only was it not functioning, it was momentarily backfiring, producing thrust out the *front*—thereby increasing the drag on that side.

The copilot, acting in a flash, decided to abort the take-off.

Now there is a standard procedure for taking off after losing an engine past V_1. The book says it can be done, and 707 pilots are required to practice it in training. The airplane should be rotated so as to reach V_2 immediately after lift-off. The gear is retracted after a positive rate of climb has been established, and V_2 speed is maintained until reaching 800 feet. Then the flaps are retracted and a climbout is made. From that point, the airplane would be landed almost normally.

But this was a split-second decision, and the man with his hands on the throttles elected to abort. Once made, they were committed to that decision; the jet engines take a few seconds to wind up power again, and by that time they would have crashed past the airport boundary.

Kadoch took over, applied reverse thrust, speed brakes, and all the foot power he could to the brakes on the wheels. The nosewheel, a little high, skipped up and down along the runway, making steering difficult. Finally it settled, and the plane began to lose speed. It stopped just short of the runway fence. The balky engine began running again. After an inspection, they resumed their trip and completed it on four healthy engines. It went into the books as an aborted takeoff.

Several years later, flying a fan-jet 707 out of Newark, New Jersey, Kadoch ran into an almost similar problem. They were fifty feet off the ground, when suddenly he said, "Look at the birds!" Ahead of them were black flecks stretching a quarter mile into the air and fifty yards across.

In a twinkling they were into the flock—which turned out to be charred bits of paper and trash, not birds at all.

If you conclude from those experiences that birds are dangerous, Kadoch will back you up. "A bird can stop an engine cold," he says. "A flock of birds can stop an airplane even colder."

Airport authorities go to great lengths to discourage bird nesting around runways, for that reason. The birds are unpredictable, and there is little the jet pilot can do during crucial takeoff and landing periods to avoid them.

The pilot can avoid other trouble, though. And Bob Kadoch spends his life avoiding airplane trouble. Don't let the perpetual grin and the joking phrases fool you; Kadoch, the TWA captain, is as serious as they come when it's time to steer away from trouble. I was with him on one trip when air traffic control tried to steer him into nasty-looking clouds. "That's not where we want to go," he said into the microphone. "That's where the buildup is; we want to go the other way." It was a little more difficult to get the new clearance, but the ground station gave in, and their new heading took them away from the turbulence.

When it involves safety, Robert A. Kadoch is a stubborn man.

CHAPTER 11

Baltimore's Friendship Airport once was called by *Life* magazine a "big, lonely" place. That was before the jet age. Today it's not so big anymore, as big airports go, and it's certainly anything but lonely. Despite the competition of nearby Dulles International, outside of adjacent Washington, D.C., Friendship is a busy place.

It was on the hectic side when Captain Bob Kadoch took over Flight 61 on a July Thursday afternoon, bound for Los Angeles. Ground crews swarmed over the Boeing 707 (model 131-B) jet, and ticket agents were kept busy getting

Training board shows jet's flight-director system.
Approach patterns are at right.

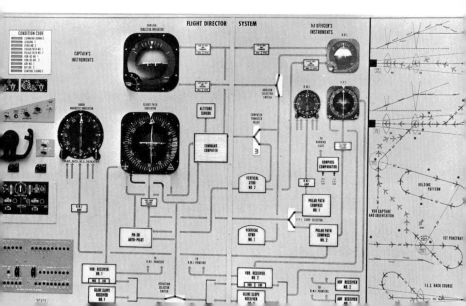

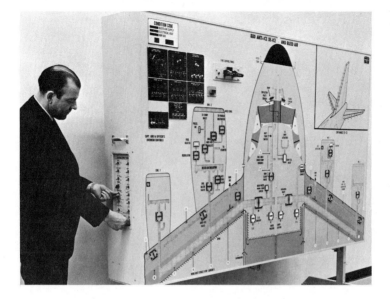

Convair 880's anti-ice systems are shown in this training board. Pilot has to know it intimately.

89 tourist-class and 14 first-class passengers seated. The load of 103 passengers was a score short of the plane's capacity, and we took on 74,000 pounds of fuel for the 3,000-mile jaunt across country.

First officer William C. (Chuck) Hasler was busy filing a flight plan; flight engineer Vernon Prather was on his walk-around check, supervising fuel loading. Kadoch, Hasler, and Prather shared fifty-eight years of TWA experience among them. For Hasler, this would be his last flight as copilot. Beginning August 1, he was to be promoted to captain, flying the Convair 880's. Kadoch brought along a camera to get a souvenir picture of the captain-to-be.

Chuck Hasler, who flew Navy dive bombers in the Pacific during World War II, was a Constellation captain when the jets came out. He had just been through the company's school in Kansas City, learning his duties aboard the 880.

107

Prather, whose first solo was in 1936, had been a TWA flight engineer since 1945. He had been pilot-qualified since 1964.

To commemorate his twentieth anniversary with the company, Prather had gotten a closely cropped crew cut. Between the haircut and the occasion of Chuck Hasler's last flight as copilot, there was plenty of built-in humor on Flight 61 that day.

But not yet. First came the business of getting the airplane into the air.

Ground power was hooked up and running when the crewmen took their places in the spacious cockpit. The last passengers filed in as they completed their initial checklist.

"Gear lever and lights."

"Down and check."

"Parking brake."

"On."

"Flight instruments."

"Check."

"Altimeters and clocks."

"Set and cross-check."

They went on down through the more than forty items, each one vital to the smooth performance of the airplane. And the flight engineer checked his twenty-five items along with them.

Then the chief crewman on the ground broke in, via intercom:

"If you're ready to pressurize the hydraulic system, Captain, we can start our engines. Clear on three and four."*

"O.K., here we go," replied Kadoch. "Pressurize," he said to Hasler, sitting in the right seat. The copilot performed his hydraulic pressurization duties quickly, and Kadoch was ready to start engines.

---

* Standard airline procedure is to start the four engines in 3, 4, 2, 1 order, leaving the left-hand engine until last, since that's the side passengers use to embark.

"Clear on three?" he asked.

"Clear on three," came the reply.

"O.K., we're starting three," said the captain. Start switches were activated, and as the r.p.m.'s built up in three, he added fuel, carefully watching his engine instruments to make certain they were functioning perfectly.

"Clear on four."

"Clear on four."

"Starting four," he said, repeating the procedure.

All ground power was disconnected; two and then one were started. The noise was barely audible in the cockpit, despite the fact that the engines were capable of 18,000 pounds of thrust each.

A hostess came up and handed them the weight-balance sheet.

"Baltimore, this is Trans World 61 at the gate, ready to taxi, IFR Los Angeles," Chuck Hasler said into his microphone.

"TWA 61 cleared to runway one-zero," came the answer. "Wind one-zero-five at seven, altimeter three-zero point zero-zero."

Their clearance to Runway 10 put them almost directly into the seven-mile-per-hour wind, blowing from 105 degrees. They started taxiing, Kadoch following the hand signals given by the crewman on the ground.

It took nearly five minutes to reach Runway 10. Meanwhile, they completed twenty more items on the checklist. Midway through the checklist, Baltimore Departure Control broke in with their IFR clearance: "Trans World 61 cleared via Baltimore to Woodbine; maintain 4,000; expect two-three-zero after Woodbine."

Hasler repeated the clearance into the microphone, while flight engineer Prather completed the checklist with Kadoch. The jet airway they were to use was out of Baltimore as far as the Woodbine checkpoint. They were to go to 4,000 feet, and after passing Woodbine they could expect to be cleared to 23,000 feet. From Woodbine, they were to head for Front Royal, Virginia.

The schedule called for a 3 P.M. departure, and at exactly 3 they started to taxi. Kadoch maneuvered the huge airplane through the maze of taxiways, steering with the little half-wheel at his left hand which controlled (via power steering) the nose gear. Then it was time to go. "Six-one, cleared for takeoff," said the impassive voice in the tower.

Flight 61 rolled down the runway quickly, and picked up speed. At 80 knots, Kadoch forsook the steering wheel for the yoke (wheel) in front of him; 80 knots is airlines-industry standard for beginning to steer with the flight controls. At 124 knots, Hasler called out "Vee-one," and moments later, "Rotate." Properly trimmed, the big jet lifts off easily. We were off the ground.

The fan-engine jet is the most powerful airliner on earth. She climbed out quickly, reaching 2,000 feet in a matter of moments, and already was traveling well over 240 knots.

"TWA 61, traffic, 11 o'clock, 2 miles eastbound," said the voice on the earphones. "No 12 o'clock," it said.

"There he is," said Hasler. "Roger, we have him," he said to the controller below.

"Sixty-one, say your airspeed and altitude," requested the voice.

"Two-eighty out of five," said Kadoch. We were doing better than 280 miles per hour, and already were well past the 5,000-foot mark. The altimeter wound up quickly. The only sound was the whoosh of the big jets far behind us, and the occasional voice from the earphones.

"Roger. Maintain two-three-zero [23,000 feet] and report out of ten," said the voice.

"Going to two-three-zero, will report out of ten," said Hasler.

Down below, patches of white clouds drifted over the East Coast. Ahead, there was nothing but clear blue sky. Flight 61 pointed her nose at it and kept climbing.

"Hey, Vern, how's that haircut feel up here? A little chilly?"

"Feels great. But *you* shouldn't talk. You don't have enough hair to talk about," the flight engineer replied.

"I guess you're right. Compared to Golden Boy Kadoch here, neither of us has any hair at all." They both laughed, and Kadoch felt obliged to answer. "Just pronounce Golden Boy right," he said, running his fingers through his blond hair.

"Sixty-one, did you file to Woodbine and Front Royal?"

"Affirmative," said Hasler. But his answer was lost in a flurry of new conversation. "Air Force . . . say again?" "O.K., maintain two-two-zero . . ."

"TWA 61, did you say you filed Woodbine, Front Royal?"

"We did file Woodbine, Front Royal," said Hasler. "We're picking up Front Royal now."

"Roger. Then proceed direct Front Royal, and maintain three-one-zero." This was to be our planned flight altitude.

"Three-one-zero, and we're just out of ten, sir," said Kadoch while Hasler jotted down the new instructions.

"Trans World 61 contact Washington radar one-two-one-point-zero [121.0 on the VHF radio]," said the voice.

"One-two-one-zero; yes, sir, and good day," said Hasler. He changed frequencies. "Washington Radar, TWA 61 with you, leaving ten for three-one."

"Roger 61. Report out of 16."

"Will report leaving 16."

"Sixty-one squawk ident." This is a signal for the flight crew to activate a device called a transponder, which enables the radar controller to identify the blip on his screen as this particular flight. We were given several "squawk codes" on the flight, and at each new radar station below, we were asked to "Squawk ident." Each time they asked, Hasler or Kadoch would press a button on the transponder, sending the coded signal below.

"Roger, radar contact," replied the voice.

"Out of 16 for three-one-zero," said Hasler.

"Contact Washington Center Radar on one-three-four-point-four," said the voice.

"Roger, one-three-four-four," Hasler answered. "Good day."

"Sixty-one out of 16 for three-one," he said.

"Roger, and radar contact," came the reply. "Report out of 24 and on reaching 31."

"Roger, will report two-four and three-one."

The big jet was climbing at 1500 feet per minute now, and traveling at 300 knots.

"TWA 61, traffic, 11 o'clock, 10 miles southbound," the voice said.

But his altitude must have been much higher or much lower than ours. We never did see him.

"Sixty-one out of 24 for 31," Hasler said.

We were past Front Royal, heading for Columbus, Ohio, 213 nautical miles west. "Leaving three for three-one," said Hasler, officially reminding Kadoch that we were at 30,000 feet.

"Trans World 61 level at three-one-zero," Hasler said. His message was confirmed.

Hasler did a quick ground-speed check, using the distance measuring equipment and the sweep second hand on the clock in front of him. We were doing 515 knots. "Better than we planned," he said. "We're getting a little tailwind component here, and we thought we were going to *lose* 45 knots. That's great."

Outside, the temperature was —45° centigrade (about a hundred degrees below zero).

We passed Columbus, and headed for the 175-mile route to Indianapolis, passing over Martinsburg. Behind us, the hostesses were showing a first-run motion picture. Below, squared-off farms covered the landscape.

It was almost 4 o'clock. A hostess came up and offered

dinner. "Not yet," said the three men on the flight deck. "But how about some iced tea?" She smiled, and disappeared back into the passenger compartment. "Hey, make that Coke for me," said Prather.

"Don't think she heard you," Kadoch said. "Hope you can survive on iced tea." But when she returned she had the Coke too.

"Trans World 61 turn right to two-seven-two," said the radio. We made an immediate right turn. "Roger, right to two-seven-two," said Kadoch. A few minutes later, the voice was back again, putting us back on our original heading. In between, we overheard the voice in conversation with an Air Force jet. The radar controller had moved us over to make way for the military plane.

We were past Indianapolis and heading for Springfield, Illinois. The plane was on autopilot; at high altitudes, the autopilot is much smoother than a man could hope to be at the controls. It anticipates changes in altitude and heading, and gently eases the 600-m.p.h. jet back onto course, imperceptibly. The altimeter hand stayed within twenty feet of 31,000, and judging by our compass, we never strayed as much as a half degree. There wasn't a bump to mar the trip so far. Even with the more-than-human autopilot running things, one live pilot must be at the controls. Hasler monitored it carefully while Kadoch went aft.

A hundred miles west of Springfield, on the route to Kansas City, we crossed the Mississippi below at Hannibal, Missouri, Mark Twain's fabled hometown. At Kansas City, Kadoch pointed out the municipal airport, almost in the heart of town, and the huge Mid-Continent International, to the northwest. "Hello, bosses," said Hasler as we passed TWA's hometown.

We headed for Salina, Kansas, 144 miles away. "Looks like we have a little weather up ahead," said Kadoch, switching on the radar set in front of him. Dead ahead, fifty miles away, was a long line of cumulus clouds, many of them

113

dark with signs of thunderstorms.

"We're going a little bit left here, Salina," said Kadoch into his microphone. "Looks slightly rough up there." He scanned the radar. The clouds showed up white; where they did, it was relatively smooth. But where there were black spots, we could expect precipitation and rough weather. We wanted to stay clear of all of it, if possible.

We detoured left a few degrees. As we crossed Alamosa, New Mexico, in the mid-Rockies, we went even farther south, maybe forty miles.

"One flight I was on once, we got way up into Canada trying to get away from a front," said Prather. "Then we went all the way south to El Paso, and then into L.A." Kadoch and Hasler wouldn't believe him. "Really did," insisted the flight engineer, "honest. All the way north, then all the way south, and then L.A."

We crossed Farmington, New Mexico, and turned north. "You'll see," said Prather. "We may have to do it this trip."

"If we did, how much fuel would we have left?" asked Hasler.

"Oh, about a pound and a half," Prather smiled.

"Well, we'd better not do it then. That's cutting it a little close. I don't want to say I goofed on my last copilot trip. I want to be a good captain, not like old Robert K. here. Look where he's taking us. Gee, it must be great to be a captain. Is it rough, Captain, I mean making those decisions and everything?"

"There's nothing as lonely as a command," said Kadoch, going along with the gag. "Decisions, decisions, decisions. Like where in the world is Los Angeles from here? Does anybody know the way?"

"Well, you see that water tank down there?" added Prather. "Just turn right at the dirt road behind it, and you'll come to a hardtop road. Turn right there . . . oh, never mind. You can't get there from here anyhow. Why don't we go back to wherever it was we were when we knew where we were? We have plenty of fuel."

"Ah, let's not give up yet. I'll recognize L.A. by the surfers," said Kadoch. "Decisions, decisions. And now my crew wants to mutiny on me. What next?"

The joking continued: "Wait, chief. We're behind you and we want you to know it. To prove it to you I'll tell you this: We are heading for Bryce Canyon, Utah. In fact, thar 'tis now. See, everybody?"

We had gone far north of our planned route. In the passenger compartment, no one could have known that we were deviating. But they might have appreciated the fact that despite vicious thunderstorms ahead, we hadn't bumped yet. It was as smooth as when we left Baltimore, hours ago.

"We're over Bryce Canyon now," said Kadoch into the microphone. "I think we've detoured almost enough. Let's head on in, shall we?"

Between the radar below and the one in the airplane, we had avoided every major buildup ahead. We were 130 miles north of Las Vegas; we circled south to avoid the last of the weather, and accepted the Jet 60 airway to Daggett, California, over San Bernadino and Ontario, and west into Los Angeles.

The steaks were eaten before we contacted Los Angeles approach control. They sent us down to 26,000, then 24,000, then 12,000. A warning horn sounded* as we reduced power.

"Ladies and gentlemen, this is the captain speaking," lied Hasler. (Then, out of the side of the mouth, while the

---

* There is a complete system of warning bells and horns on the Boeings. An intermittent bell signifies that the plane's speed is too high; a steady bell signals an engine fire. One intermittent horn tells that the cabin is losing pressure (it works in the air only, and can be silenced). Another sounds if the plane starts its takeoff roll with the speed brake activated. A third sounds if flaps aren't in the proper position, and a fourth if the stabilizer trim is off. A steady horn sounds (and can be silenced) if power is cut without the gear being lowered, or if more than 30 degrees of flaps are lowered without the gear being down, or if the gear handle is not down and locked.

PA system was switched off momentarily: "You don't mind if I practice using that word, do you, Bob?")

"No, go right ahead, feel free. You've been practicing on my airplane, using my fuel and everything. Why not my name? Oh my, the perils of command. Such a rebellious crew. Wait till we reach Hong Kong. They'll never believe this when we reach port."

"Not enough fuel for Hong Kong," said Prather. "How about Guam?"

Hasler continued on the public-address system: "We've had to detour around a little here to avoid some nasty weather. But we expect to arrive in Los Angeles pretty much according to schedule. The Los Angeles weather is good, the temperature is 72°, and we'll be going in quickly now. Thank you."

We were down to 9,000 feet, and heading for 7,000. "Gross weight, 157,500," said Prather. Hasler calculated the approach speeds, and also how much power we'd need if we had to go around again at Los Angeles.

We switched over to the tower frequency, and Prather began reading the before-landing checklist.

"Thirty flaps," said Kadoch. All the humor was gone. This was serious business. "Thirty flaps," answered Hasler. "Gear down." "Gear," came the reply. "Forty flaps," said Kadoch. We were turning base, and only 1500 feet off the ground. Prather was reading the last part of the prelanding checklist.

"Landing gear."

"Down and three greens."

"Yaw damper."

"Check."

"No-smoke sign."

"On."

"Anti-skid."

We were fifty feet off the ground. Kadoch eased the yoke back as we roared in, flying at well over 100 knots. The gear greased onto the runway. His right hand reached out and activated the speed brakes—the huge spoilers on the wings. We slowed quickly, without reverse thrust, and were quickly down to taxiing speed.

"On at three-six," said Prather. It was 7:36 Eastern time, only 4:36 Pacific time. We were two minutes behind schedule. We taxied quickly to the gate. As we headed in toward the platform, Kadoch kept his eyes on two red lights. When he had them aligned, he turned right, watching a new set of three lights. When the middle light came into focus, he stopped the airplane and shut down the engines.

We completed the secure-cockpit checklist, accepted ground power, and got out behind the passengers. We walked around to the front of the airplane and looked at the nose gear. It was resting directly on the painted line that showed precisely where we were to park.

"Easier than my sedan," said Kadoch, grinning.

CHAPTER 12

Landing systems are getting better all the time. The pilot has his choice of a normal instrument landing system (ILS), an autopilot approach directed by a computer on board, one directed by a ground controller, or a combination of them all.

One of the most exciting is the PAR (precision approach radar)* landing, in which a ground controller talks the pilot down. I sat in a 707 cockpit and watched one performed at San Francisco's International Airport. The captain placed a pillow in front of the windshield on the copilot's side (he'll be doing this landing), forcing him to rely exclusively on the instruments in front of him, and on the voice in his earphones.

Flight 21 was at 7,000 feet when the controller made arrangements for the approach.

"If no transmissions are received for two minutes, abandon the approach and make a normal ILS approach," he said. Then: "21, say your airspeed."

"We're now 230," said the copilot.

"Maintain that for the next ten miles," ordered the controller.

"Roger."

"21, descend to 6,000."

* Also known as a GCA—Ground-Controlled Approach.

"21, descend and maintain 4,000."

"Four thousand, TWA 21, and we're now 220."

"21, traffic at 12 o'clock, on glide path. . . . Descend and maintain 2,000."

"Change frequencies now to one-two-eight-point five."

"21, traffic at 9 o'clock eastbound. Turn left to a heading of three-one-zero."

"Perform your cockpit check here."

"Cockpit check completed," said the captain, after a few moments.

"Turn left to two-eight-zero. You are turning final."

"Turn right to two-eight-five. . . . If no transmissions are received for five seconds, abandon the approach . . ."

"Maintain altitude. You are eight miles from touch-down."

 "Seven and one half miles from touchdown; begin descent."

"Gear down," ordered the copilot; landing gear is lowered.

"You are on the glide path, seven miles from touchdown. Adjust your rate of descent."

"Turn left to two-eight-zero."

"Turn right to two-eight-two. You are twenty-five feet below the glide path. Adjust your rate of descent."

"You are five miles from touchdown."

"You are a hundred feet below the glide path, four and one half miles from touchdown."

"You are on course two-eight-two, still a hundred feet before glide path, four miles from touchdown."

"Turn left to two-eight-zero. You are three and one half miles from touchdown."

"Turn left to two-seven-eight. You are fifty feet right of the course."

"You are three miles from touchdown, on glide path."

"Turn to two-eight-zero. You are twenty-five feet above the glide path, two and one quarter miles from touchdown."

"You are two miles from touchdown."

"You are fifty feet above glide path."

"You are one and one half miles from touchdown, twenty-five feet above glide path."

". . . On glide path . . . fifteen feet above."

"Turn left to two-seven-niner."

"Turn right to two-eight-two. On course, on glide path, one half mile from touchdown." (Pillow removed here.)

"On course, on glide path. . . . Twenty-five feet to the right of center line. Touchdown . . ."

The controller was off by a few feet; we touched down almost exactly on the centerline of the runway, and came to a smooth stop.

The controller does it by means of two radars, one showing the plane's on-course heading, and the other its rate of descent. The proper rate of descent is along a 3-degree grade leading to the threshold of the runway. Frequent changes of heading are required because of winds and to correct for earlier errors. The controller's voice remains calm; even when we were 100 feet off our glide path he didn't raise it. The pilot, watching his instruments, must react instantaneously to the controller's commands. His movements are deft ones.

Without the controller's voice ringing in my own set of earphones, I would have guessed we were making a normal visual approach. A hundred passengers on board must have thought so too.

PART
III

CHAPTER 13

The single-engine jet dashes in for a landing at 130 knots, wheels and flaps down. It turns from base onto final, and maintains a long, shallow rate of descent. It is less than a quarter mile from touchdown. Scores of eyes watch as it closes the gap.

Nose a little high, it begins to flatten out its angle of attack. Abruptly, it is down, still traveling at well over 100 knots. Before contact, the pilot adds full power, and the engine shrieks. Its tail hook latches on to a thick steel cable, and the Navy fighter lurches to a halt, bouncing on its nosewheel. Inside the cockpit, the pilot is thrown forward against his shoulder straps. His head bounces ahead of him, and his eyeballs press against eyelids.

The airplane comes to a stop—300 feet from touchdown. The tail hook is raised, the cable pulled back, and the plane taxis out of the way. Right behind, just a half minute behind, is another fighter.

A few yards away from the scene, a third fighter roars its engines, while crewmen hitch a cable to its underbelly. The pilot performs his run-up check, salutes smartly, and braces for the shock. An officer outside raises his arm, lowers it, and touches the deck. A man pushes a button, and there is an additional roar. The pilot's head is snapped back against the headrest, his shoulders forced tightly against the seat. From a zero start, he'll be doing 160 knots within 250 feet

—and he'll be airborne.

This is normal operation aboard a modern attack aircraft carrier. The same critical jet speeds are vital here, as they are when TWA lands its 707's. But instead of a runway 10,000 feet long, this one is a thirtieth of that distance. And there is no takeoff runway, just steam catapults capable of 100,000 pounds of thrust.

The reasoning is simple: an aircraft carrier is nothing more than a floating airport. Jets, which normally need runways 7,000 feet or longer, obviously can't afford anything that luxurious at sea. So the Navy gives them the next best thing—a push to get started, and a pull to stop them.

Launching and recovering speedy jets at sea is unbeliev-

*An F–8 Crusader grabs the first wire in landing
aboard carrier U.S.S. Coral Sea. Third wire
landing is ideal.*

able, even after you've seen it. (It's all the more incomprehensible after you've seen the fast jets land and take off from conventional runways.) Airplanes aren't supposed to start that fast, and they take much more room to stop; anybody who has ever flown knows that. But here they are, a hundred and more of them crammed onto a single ship, flitting into the sky in all sorts of weather and somehow coming down again. If you didn't know better, you'd feel safe in accusing the United States Government of trickery.

Consider the launch: I sat through the catapult procedure, in a fast attack bomber. I was strapped in across the lap and down from the shoulders to the waist. I was further restricted by a Mae West life preserver, with all its equipment, including shark repellent and emergency signal radio; by the traditional hard hat, complete with earphones and microphones; by a flight suit and boots; by a tightly fitting oxygen mask; by a seat that left me less room than I get in the Volkswagen at home.

Yet I might have been held by a loose rubber band, for all the shock-absorbent effectiveness I got.* I was sitting in the radar operator's seat of an A-3 bomber, facing aft. I was pushed forward with such force by the catapult that I thought I'd leave a permanent indentation in the cabinet ahead of me. The shock and roar lasted for several long seconds, and were displaced by an eerie silence—as quiet as the cruising 707. We had left the ship, and were climbing safely ahead of it. I tentatively leaned back, and was surprised to discover that I still could.

A few minutes later we were ready for shock number two —the recovery via tail hook and steel cable. We descended slowly, as slowly as our stalling speed would let us. We crossed the fantail of the ship, then added power in a screaming burst of turbines—and at almost the same mo-

---

* The shock of launch and recovery is so great that carrier planes are built to withstand a drop from a two-story building and remain structurally intact. By comparison, the same jets, if used by the Air Force, would need structuring less than a third that rugged.

An A–4 is launched for an attack.

ment engaged the little steel cable that would enable us to stop. Now I went backward, and with such force that I again wondered about whether I'd survive. I don't know how far that seat behind me actually gave with the strain, but it felt as if it didn't budge a centimeter. Vision left me momentarily as we crunched to a halt some 300 feet after catching the cable. I remember being mildly surprised that nothing had gone wrong—that this was standard, normal, everyday procedure. "You mean," I asked myself, "that the catapult didn't throw us at twice the thrust, and that we didn't stop inside of 30 feet, rather than 300?"

"Nope," I answered. "This is the way it's done as a matter of course. This is the way they fly these things off the ship, and back onto it again."

And I thought of something else: imagine *trying to fly an airplane* while all this is going on!

I have flown in turbulent weather* many times, and I can guarantee you that it's twice as hard trying to hold a heading or maintain an altitude in bumpy weather as in calm skies. I can imagine what it takes to maneuver a touchy jet safely while undergoing this kind of strain. (Of course, there is little maneuvering to do while you are actually being catapulted, or recovered. But think of the pressures involved while you are approaching the carrier deck, knowing full well that if you do it right, you're in for all that shock. And I wonder how much courage it takes to sit there in the cockpit and salute the catapult officer, knowing that your time-honored salutation is a signal for The Man with the Biggest Thumb in the World to kick you upstairs. "It's quite a boot in the butt, isn't it?" asked a squadron commander when I had survived my first cat shot.)

Private flying is fun. Commercial flying is serious business that can be fun if you go about doing your job the right way. But flying those jets off and on carriers is nothing but the epitome of skill. If there is a flying job in the world that's tougher, I haven't seen it. If there is one that requires a higher degree of technical efficiency, coupled with more raw courage and sheer airmanship, it's been eluding me so far. If carrier flying today isn't the world's most difficult aviation job, it'll have to do until the real thing comes along.

The surprise of carrier aviation is that there are human beings involved—not prestressed robots. Here are men with the same interest in flying, with the same number of eyes, feet, and hands; but men who have developed a consum-

* Not "air pockets," because there isn't any such thing. Thermals, downdrafts, and other currents account for turbulence.

mate skill and then honed it to perfection. To them, practice is life insurance.

A high-ranking naval officer told me that only once in a great while does the Navy find a man who can survive all its testing and training and then fail to make a carrier pilot. "Sometimes, very seldom, we find a guy that we have almost to shoot out of the air to get down," he said, as we cruised aboard a carrier off the Virginia Capes. "He winds up flying somewhere else, of course."

But that doesn't mean that Navy carrier pilots aren't living in a state of perpetual respect for the hazards of their trade. I lived with them and ate with them, talking to them by the hour. I never met one of them who didn't exhibit a healthy, fearlike confidence (but *not* fear itself) in his work. They were all afraid, to be certain. I don't think any man who stops to think about the hazards of driving—much less flying, much less fast flying, much less carrier flying—can help being afraid. But their being afraid somehow didn't translate into what we think of as fear. There wasn't the panic that goes with fear, or the lack of rational thought. There was rather an aura of respect. "These things can kill you," one pilot told me. "But they can be flown." Implicit was the promise: "We'll fly them."

It's that same mastery over machine that makes these men operate the way they do. It can be done, and it will.

One young pilot shared hamburgers and coffee with me the day before he was to qualify for night operations aboard a carrier. He spent a half hour telling me how dangerous night operations could be. He told me how easy it is to lose your sense of feel for the carrier deck, how wild a sight it is to roar down into nothingness. But when I asked him how ready he felt, he grinned and held up a thumb in the historic aviation sign for "Let's go!"

We talked for a while longer. I was frankly trying to probe into the mind of a man who willingly risks his neck in this nerve-stretching job, and I told him so.

"Oh, I meant every word I said about the danger," he replied. "But I also believe that we are the best-trained men in the world, riding the best ship, flying the best airplanes, and working with the best crews. If we can't do it, nobody can. And I don't want to sound as though I'm waving flags, but I think we're real preservers of peace. If anybody wants to tangle with Uncle Sam's Navy—including all the fire-power that he can fly off his decks—he's willing to try. I think the fact that we exist this way, trained and primed, is enough to make nations think twice about war. We don't talk war around here. We talk peace; and to ensure it, we're ready for anything—even war, if it comes right down to that."

And how about the actual dangers involved?

"They're down to a minimum, and getting better every minute," he said. "There aren't any unnecessary chances that are taken aboard an aircraft carrier. You'll see that in the next day or so when we start flying. There is hazardous work, but there are also men by the thousands who work to reduce the hazards. We're not thrill-seeking daredevils here, but men getting a job done right. Many of us have families, children. I don't think these men are trying to get themselves killed. The first thing you have to know about this work is that it *can* kill you. When you realize that, you're in a much better position to stay alive."

CHAPTER 14

Essentially, flying an airplane onto a carrier deck is like flying one onto any other runway: you merely set up the right glide angle, keep it lined up with the runway, and aim for a spot—except that in carrier flying, the spot you're aiming for is only a couple of hundred feet long. If you miss it, you don't land on that try.

Think it's difficult to aim for those four steel cables? Then think about this: the carrier pilot really aims for *a single cable* (the third one), less than two inches in diameter!

Any number of things can go wrong; the pilot's job is to make sure that they don't, or—barring that—to make certain that their failure doesn't hurt.

The most common mistake, as you've no doubt guessed, is missing that one single cable. Sometimes you hit the first cable (which means you're lower than you should have been), or the fourth one (you're too high), or cable number two (almost perfect, but not quite). The second most common error: missing the cables altogether. The tail hook sometimes skips ("bolters"), and you have to go around again. Or, once in a while, it doesn't even touch down.

For these reasons, the jet carrier pilot adds full power just moments before he touches down. It takes the jet engines a while to wind up again, and he wants good thrust behind him if he has to go through it a second time. Watching a bolter is like watching a controlled near-accident. You know it happened, and you know how dangerous it's supposed to be, but everything somehow looks as if it came out all right.

Watching the tail hook snare a cable and stop that shrieking bird is like seeing a film stop before your eyes. The airplane is moving—fast. Suddenly it's not moving. It happens so quickly that you have to turn your head and watch the next one to believe the first. The airplane looks too fast and powerful, and the cable looks too skinny to make it stop. But somehow they stop, by the dozens.

At peak daytime efficiency, the carrier crews can land an airplane every thirty-five seconds. (They can launch four a minute.) The frequency of landings is cut down somewhat at night (one every ninety seconds), but the crews can grope their way around a pitch-dark deck, in fifty-knot winds, and still manage to recover airplanes.

*Skyhawk dips slightly after launch
from carrier U.S.S. Ranger.*

The hangar deck of the U.S.S. Ranger
replete with ammunition

Beyond piloting, almost every aviation-connected job aboard an aircraft carrier is a tough one. The landing signal officer holds the life of the pilot and the value of the airplane (up to $12 million) in his hands. The deck crewmen manning recovery stations and catapults have to work with precision or risk pilot and airplane. The people in operations have to schedule aircraft departures and arrivals in a maze of details. Men who run the electronic welter in the ship's innards are experts. The entire ship's crew—fully manned, there are 4500 of them—is a meshed movement dedicated to keeping the floating airport working.

The carrier has everything the land airport has, and more. There is a control tower; there are maintenance shops; there are fueling crews; there are armament experts (nuclear too); there are fire fighters and paper handlers. And there are cooks and bakers, barbers and carpenters, electricians and boiler men, typists and laundrymen, clerks and cobblers, chaplains, dentists, accountants, and doctors. Their average age: less than twenty.

The U.S.S. *Forrestal*, the ship I boarded to learn about carrier aviation, is over 1,000 feet long, 250 feet wide, and displaces 78,000 tons with fuel, weapons, planes, and men aboard. Despite her size, she can move through all but the roughest seas at more than 30 knots. Her flight deck covers four acres.

To move aircraft between the flight deck and hangar bays, *Forrestal* has four huge elevators, each capable of lifting an 80,000-pound load to the flight deck in less than five seconds.

The ship carries planes ranging in size from the A-4 Skyhawk, the smallest military jet in operation, to the A-3 Skywarrior, the heavy attack bomber that is the largest ever flown from carriers. In between are the F-4 Phantoms, all-weather day or night interceptors that can climb to 30,000 feet in little more than a minute, and the F-8 Crusaders, which can buzz around the sky at better than 1100 m.p.h. In-flight refueling helps extend the range of the planes.

And there are the angels—the helicopters, which Navy men call "helos" (pronounced "hee-lows")—whose job is rescue and occasional cargo operations.

The primary job is keeping airplanes flyable, but there are other tasks as well. The galleys cook and serve more than 15,000 meals a day at sea, involving two tons of meat, 1,000 loaves of bread, and 9,000 pounds of vegetables.

It is the size of the ship itself that impresses the first-time visitor. If turned on end, *Forrestal* would reach the 80th floor of the Empire State Building. She is wide enough to berth both the SS *United States* and the SS *America* on her flight deck. From her keel to the top of her (hinged) mast, she is as tall as a 25-story building.

There are more than 2,000 compartments in the ship. The entire ship is air-conditioned with water-cooled forced air. Each of the ship's two anchors weighs thirty tons; one link in the anchor chain weighs 360 pounds. Each of her four propellers is 22 feet in diameter. It takes 300,000 gallons of paint yearly to keep her shipshape—enough to paint 30,000 homes. There is a library with more than 3500 volumes, and more than 800 dial telephones aboard.

In short, she is a city housing nearly 5,000 people which boasts a modern airfield.

The ship has two runways; in the words of one squadron commander, "It took the navies of the world a long time to think of this design, and yet it's probably the simplest idea and the most valuable one in the history of floating aviation."

In World War II, pilots had a choice of making a good landing or crashing into a barricade erected to protect the rest of the ship's airplanes, parked forward on the carrier deck. *Forrestal* and other modern carriers have an angled deck running toward the port side, plus the main deck running fore and aft. Airplanes can be landed on the angled deck while others are being catapulted up forward. If a pilot misses an approach, he merely goes around again. If a crash is unavoidable, at least it doesn't endanger the other airplanes and men on board.

The recovery system consists of the four cables, with engines for a capacity of 60,000 pounds at 115 knots. The engines and wires have a breaking strength of 171,000 pounds.

The catapults—two forward and two on the angled deck —are powered by steam, heated to 585° at a pressure of 600 pounds per square inch. The two angle-deck catapults can launch 48,000-pound airplanes at 125 m.p.h. The two forward can launch 57,000-pound airplanes at the same speed.

The arresting cables not only sit there—they also tug at the airplane, at precise precalculated pressures. When an airplane is turning onto final, it is identified and the information relayed to the arresting gear crews belowdecks. They set the gear to stop that particular airplane. The strength it takes to stop one of the heavy attack bombers would tear the tail hook (and maybe part of the airplane) from one of the ship's little mosquito-like Phantoms. *Forrestal* officers told me that when the ship was newer, several airplanes were lost because *two* cables were caught on landings. A plane's tail hook would grab a cable, skip upward, and catch a second cable on the way down. Engineers spent many weeks aboard ship to determine how to respace the cables.

The catapults, too, are preset for different airplanes. At top power, they could throw your family sedan a half mile

A Skyraider hurtles down the catapult while flight deck crewman (center) monitors instruments.

or more into the ocean. But even all that power isn't enough to get airplanes started, or to stop them. In addition, the ship must turn into the wind and cruise along at a good pace in order to add more wind across her decks. At 30 knots' cruising speed, she adds 30 knots of airspeed to an airplane on a catapult, and slows an approaching plane by just that much too. If there is a healthy breeze blowing across the sea in addition to that, so much the better. For it takes all that man can muster to make modern air operations practical in the middle of an ocean.

CHAPTER 15

"Flight quarters. All hands man your flight quarters stations." It's time aboard a huge attack carrier to launch aircraft, and scores of men appear on the flight deck.

There are ninety minutes to go, but they're going to be a busy ninety minutes. The men are dressed in brightly colored jerseys, either red, green, blue, brown, white, yellow or checkered. The color code tells you their specialty at a glance. They wear Mickey Mouse sound helmets and special suction shoes. Green shirts with large C's stenciled front and back are the cat crewmen. The letter distinguishes them from the green-shirted arresting gear crew, identified by an A.

Scattered about the deck are petty officers and commissioned officers in yellow jerseys; regardless of rank, these are the elite—the catapult officer, flight deck officer, aircraft handling officer, plane directors, and assistants. During air operations, a signal from a man in a yellow jersey is an unquestionable order, obeyed by everyone from the senior pilot to the newest crewman.

A medical corpsman, wearing a white jersey with a red cross, stands by. Another man climbs into an asbestos hot suit. Both of them are in the rescue business.

A few blue shirts (the men who push aircraft, carry chocks and heavy chain tie-downs) are busy during this crucial preflight period. Red-shirted fueling crews tote heavy hoses around the deck. At each plane is a brown-shirted plane captain. One bird is his responsibility. When it flies, he preflights it. When a corrosive accumulation of salt builds up on the plane, he washes it. He sees that it is securely fastened to the deck with at least nine chain tie-downs. When it is moved, he sits in the cockpit and rides the brakes. During flight quarters he may leave it only if relieved by another brown shirt. When there's a lull, he can get forty winks—provided that he curls up in the cockpit or on the wing.

The days when aviators simply kicked the tires and lighted the fires are gone forever, and life is far more complicated. Maintenance men are specialists these days in everything from hydraulics to radar to ejection seats. Major aircraft repairs are done below on the hangar deck; minor repairs are performed wherever the plane happens to be when spotted. Last-minute minor difficulties are corrected by troubleshooters, sometimes while the bird is on the cat waiting to be launched.

I saw a plane land nose high, crunch forward, and blow out its nosewheel on impact. Crewmen changed the tire with the efficiency of automobile racing pit crews.

Now, as launch time grows near, the tempo picks up. Using a printed checklist the brown shirt moves slowly around the airplane, pulling, tugging, pressing, and making neat little X's. As he ducks under the tail, he sees an accumulation of thin, reddish liquid. He takes some in his hand and sniffs it. Hydraulic fluid. The word is passed down the line, and green-shirted hydraulics experts converge on the airplane, look it over and shake their heads.

Throughout the ship, status boards are changed; the plane is down for hydraulic leak. In flight deck control, two-dimensional models for each airplane are positioned on a mock-up of the hangar and flight decks. The model representing the downed airplane is turned red side up. The aircraft handling officer studies it for a moment, confers

138

*The Skyhawk is readied for launch
aboard carrier U.S.S. Hancock.*

with the squadron maintenance chief, and steps out to the
flight deck. "Strike 103 down number three elevator," he
orders. Minutes later, a tiny truck (mule) gets ready to
tow 103. Within minutes, another plane is brought up and
put into 103's position. On the hangar deck, men are already
tearing into 103. They should have it ready by the second
launch.

Down belowdecks, in the ready room, pilots in bright
orange flight suits are ready for briefing. Weather information is relayed to the ready room via teletype and recorded
on clear plexiglass boards by phone talkers using grease
pencils. Ranges and bearings to "bingo" (alternate) fields
are also listed. Now comes the command, "Pilots, man your
planes. . . ." Airborne, the pilots may be speedy characters,
but now they are burdened with G suits, pistols, ammo,
Mae Wests, maps, flight cards, clipboards, hard hats, and

139

various other paraphernalia.

The flight deck is fully manned. Steam wisps up around the catapult shuttles. Pilots approach their birds, check briefly with their plane captains, and conduct their own pre-flight inspections. Last-minute checks completed, pilots are strapped in. On deck, sound helmets and goggles are snapped into place, the ship turns into the breeze, and soon a 35-knot wind is billowing down the deck.

"Start engines."

The whine of jet starters soon changes to a roar as the fuel begins to burn. The cat officer takes his place, arms folded against his chest, facing aft and leaning backward against the wind. From now on, all signals are made by hand and the most crucial by the cat officer. He is not about to risk scratching his nose.

"Stand by to launch aircraft."

The cat officer faces the starboard cat, unfolds his hands, and signals for tension on the bridle. The shuttle inches forward. The officer holds two fingers over his head, hesitates, then rotates his hand rapidly. The pilot pushes the throttle forward; his afterburner cuts in. After a quick run-up check, the pilot turns his head slightly toward the cat officer and snaps a salute. And then he's off.

Around the cat, the air is filled with steam and the hot acrid stench of burning jet fuel. As each aircraft taxis into the standby position, spreading its foldable wings, flight deck troubleshooters in checkered shirts leave their protected positions. In the midst of the inferno they check the wing locks, tail hooks, and external gear.

All over the flight deck, the checking is constant. Each man has an assignment, and his job must be done properly or else. Half a billion dollars' worth of airplanes can be catapulted into the air today, and it takes months of precision training to see that it's done safely.

Then, of course, comes that other task: getting the birds back home again.

CHAPTER 16

It would be bending the truth somewhat to say that landing a fast jet aboard an aircraft carrier is a trick done with mirrors. It's tricky, all right; and mirrors (in reality, lenses) are the key to it all.

It is the Fresnel lens system aboard a carrier that tells the pilot where he is in relation to the ship's deck. Lights projected through precision lenses give him a glide path to follow, and will lead him to cable three. It is the same angle of glide path (3°) used by commercial airports.

The approaching pilot comes into the carrier's traffic pattern at 800 feet from aft of the ship and on her starboard side. A mile or so beyond the ship (depending on where the preceding plane is), the pilot turns left into a downwind leg. At this point he dirties up the airplane (extends gear and flaps), flying at 600 feet and maybe a mile and a quarter from the ship. Then he turns left again, onto a base leg, and begins his final descent. During the last half of his turn (it's actually a base and final all rolled into a 180° turn), he picks up an image—called a "meatball"—in the Fresnel lens.* His job from then on in is to keep the bright orange ball centered during his descent to the deck. Alongside the meatball image are rows of green lights. If the glide angle is correct, the meatball stays on the row with

* There are alternate approach systems too, but the basic one is the fairly recent Fresnel lens.

141

PLANE FACTS ABOUT CARRIERS

Before recovery, the ship speeds up and turns into the wind to enable plane to land at a lower (slower) relative speed.

During last half of aircraft's 180° turn, pilot picks up meatball image in Fresnel Lens and maintains it on reference line to establish his rate of descent as he lines up angled deck visually.

Planes in the landing pattern fly one and one-half to two and one-quarter miles abeam of the ship and at 600 feet while slowing to landing speeds.

When incoming aircraft is abeam of the ship, the pri-fly officer readies crew and calls 'heads up.'

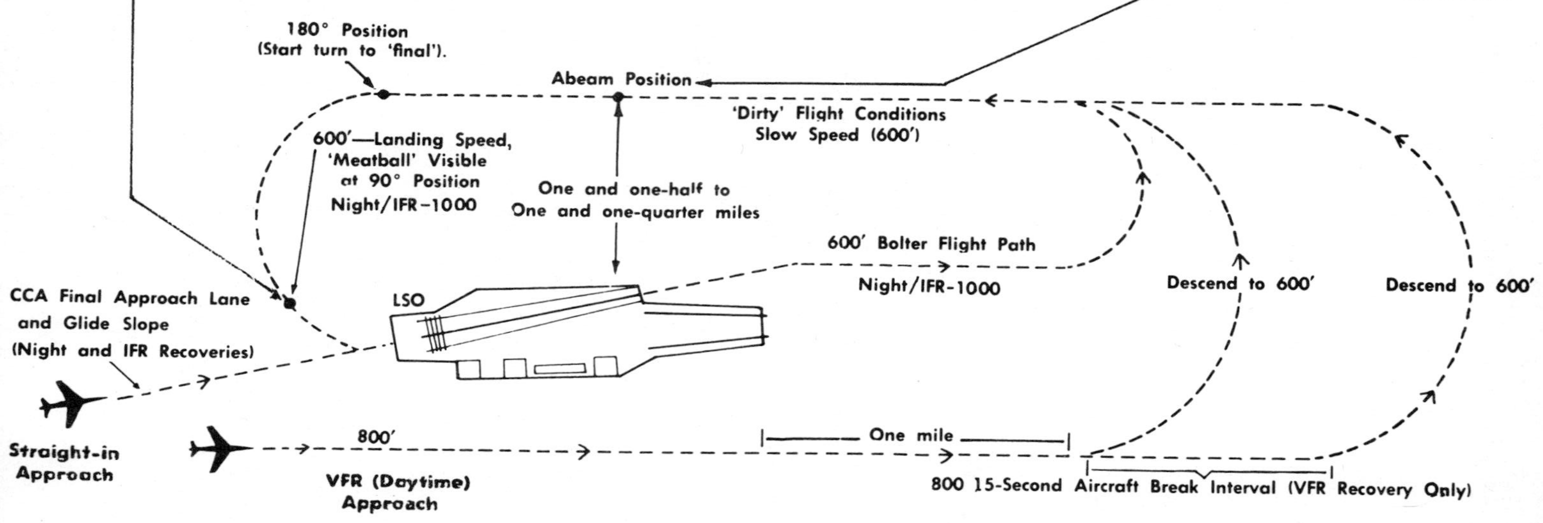

Descend to 600'

Descend to 600'

Descend to 600'

'Dirty' Flight Conditions
Slow Speed (600')

600' Bolter Flight Path
Night/IFR-1000

Abeam Position

One and one-half to
One and one-quarter miles

One mile

800 15-Second Aircraft Break Interval (VFR Recovery Only)

180° Position
(Start turn to 'final').

600'—Landing Speed,
'Meatball' Visible
at 90° Position
Night/IFR-1000

LSO

800'

VFR (Daytime)
Approach

CCA Final Approach Lane
and Glide Slope
(Night and IFR Recoveries)

Straight-in
Approach

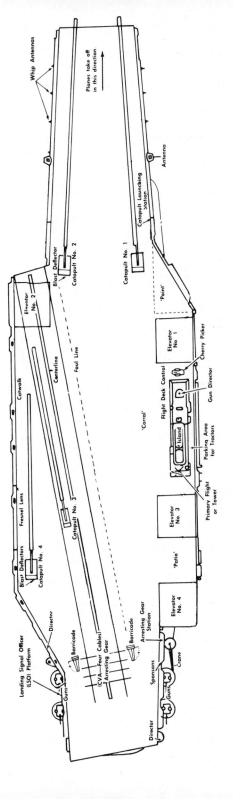

Whip Antennas

Planes take off in this direction.

Antenna

Catapult Launching Station

Catapult No. 1

Catapult No. 2

Blast Deflector

Elevator No. 2

Catapult No. 3

Centerline

Foul Line

Catwalk

Fresnel Lens

Blast Deflectors

Catapult No. 4

Director

Barricade

Four Cables
Arresting Gear

Barricade

Arresting Gear Station

Landing Signal Officer (LSO) Platform

Guns

Director

Sponsons

Guns

Crane

Elevator No. 4

'Patio'

Elevator No. 3

'Corral'

Primary Flight or Tower

Parking Area for Tractors

Gun Director

Cherry Picker

Elevator No. 1

Flight Deck Control

'Island'

'Point'

Landing pattern and carrier details are shown in these sketches, prepared for Naval personnel career publication All Hands.

Prepared by ALL HANDS Magazine

the green. If he's high, the meatball appears high. If he's low, it drops lower. If he gets precariously low, the orange meatball drops to the lowest part of the lens, and shows up bloodred.

Also mounted on the lens system are rows of red lights. In case of a bad approach, the lights are set flashing, and the pilot goes around again.

The visual approach is made with the help of the landing signal officer (LSO), who monitors instruments and the pilot's radio frequencies to keep in constant touch with the airplane. At a glance, the LSO can tell the velocity of the wind across the ship's deck, the pitch and roll of the ship, the speed of the airplane coming at him, and its relation to the glide path.

The LSO holds a telephone in one hand, linking him by radio to the pilot, and a light switch in the other hand, controlling the wave-off lights of the Fresnel lenses. The Fresnel wave-off lights are set up on a "dead man" system—they begin flashing if something should happen to the LSO.

The LSO also has three other aids to help him land the airplane safely. First there is his intimate knowledge of the airplane, coupled with his experience at that position. He knows, almost instinctively, what the airplane silhouette *looks like* when it's on the glide path. And mounted on the nose of the airplane itself are three lights set vertically and in different colors. The middle one, bright green, lights up when the plane's speed is perfect. The top one, amber, lights when the plane is too fast. The bottom one, red, lights when it's too slow. By watching the airplane and its lights, he can tell in a moment whether the approach is right.

He has only seconds in which to get the pilot to correct his approach. By the time he relays his advice, and the pilot reacts to it, the airplane is even farther off target.

The LSO station is also hooked into the ship's closed-circuit television system called PLAT, for pilot landing aid

*The lighted Fresnel lens system gives plane
a target for shipboard touchdown.*

television. The TV system records each takeoff and landing
on magnetic tape and relays it to TV sets over the ship. Two
TV cameras are set into the deck, on the center line. They
point their eyes relentlessly at the oncoming airplane, and
in the center of the lens is a set of cross hairs. In pilots'
ready rooms below, you can tell how good the approach is
by seeing whether the plane is centered in the cross hairs.

The primary purpose of the PLAT system is to allow
senior officers to watch air operations without going on the
flight deck. But it is also used as a training aid; films are
played back, and pilots can watch their own landings.

I sat in a ready room while the system was recording
landings made topside. A pilot made an approach, and was
slightly off the center line; he looked as if he was going to
be able to correct in time, but the pilots in the room all
said simultaneously, "Wave off," and they were right. "You
couldn't see enough of his tail there," one of them said.
"He was much too high, and going higher."

A high approach is the beginner's most common mistake. Without the lens—or even with it—the neophyte carrier pilot senses that he is much too low. His most frequent tendency is to go in high—too high—knowing that in altitude there is safety.

Another pilot problem is caused by the design of some airplanes. In one particular model, the cockpit is far forward of the nose gear. When the pilot taxis onto one of the ship's elevators, he is riding directly above the ocean far below, while his nosewheel is still maybe five feet behind its proper position. A deck crewman signals him to taxi farther forward, but as he looks down, all he can see is swirling sea. "It takes a lot of guts to accept that crewman's word for it that you're not going to tumble into the ocean," said one pilot. "What usually happens is that the pilot will ease the throttle forward bit by delicate bit, while holding onto the brakes."

Another problem comes from the jolt the pilot takes on recovery and launch. Tires are good for about thirteen landings. A human being can only take so much of that at a time, and the Navy wisely limits a qualifying pilot to no more than ten arrested landings or three qualification flights (of not more than an hour each in the landing pattern) in one 24-hour period. Nor may a pilot spend more than eight hours in the cockpit during one 24-hour period.

"There is, after all, a limit to this," one squadron's command told me. "We're not trying to kill these men by fatiguing them to death."

To qualify as a jet carrier pilot, after school and simulated landings on land, the pilot must make two touch-and-go landings, plus ten arrested landings, in the daytime; and six arrested landings at night. Once qualified, the pilot is considered current only for six months. Past six months, he must make four day and two night arrested landings; past twelve months he must qualify over again.

Before a pilot can qualify at night, he must make two

U.S.S. Ranger *pilots await briefing
in ready room.*

landings and one launch during daylight—within flying range of a shore base.

The trickiest one is a night landing aboard a darkened ship. All the usual difficulties are compounded by the fact that the pilot has no extra vision to help him out. He sees a tiny row of landing lights, plus the Fresnel lights, and the rest is sheer blackness.

A young pilot put it this way: "You know the ship's deck is there, but your senses tell you otherwise. There are those lights and nothing more. It's like landing in a hallway after the lights burned out, and using candlepower as a substitute.

"You get this deep feeling of nothingness—empty runway. You either have complete confidence in your equipment or you're lost before you start. If ever a pilot had to rely on his gauges and his fellowman, this is the time.

"And if the deck happens to be pitching a bit to top it all off..."

That's one of the biggest worries aboard ship. Stabilizing gyros keep the Fresnel lights accurate despite pitch and roll of the ship, but it's quite a feeling to approach the deck and find it moving out from under you. Especially when your target is a skinny little wire down there in the dark someplace.

POSTSCRIPT

Pilots are getting better all the time, and so is their equipment. Omni, once a wealthy man's navigation aid, is almost standard equipment on most light planes these days. The complicated SCAT (speed control) systems on airliners and military jets weren't there a decade ago. A few years back, nobody even dreamed of everyday, workable computers, no less computers small enough and dependable enough to put on airplanes. Yet they are there today, by the thousands.

Late in 1964, some time before this book was written, a pilot leaned back in a jet and relaxed while an automatic landing system headed him for an approach to Dulles International Airport near Washington. The pilot selected his heading, switched on a computer, and sat back with everyone else to enjoy the show. With no more directions from the pilot, the computer directed the plane to the localizer beam, put it on a glide path, constantly corrected altitude, rate of descent and speed, and generally did everything a human pilot could have done—only better. Just before touchdown, the system raised the plane's nose, closed the throttles, and let it slide gently onto the runway.

A Government aviation official aboard the airplane called it a "major breakthrough."

Will it displace pilots?

Everybody who should know says it will not. Far from it; pilots will have to be on board for a long time to come.

And more pilots are needed today than ever before. Aviation started slowly, picked up steam quickly, and now is roaring full throttle into the twenty-first century. It is big business, and getting bigger.

Civil aviation (nonmilitary and noncommercial) is a huge and growing segment involving business as well as pleasure flying. Companies that used to wince at having to buy airplane tickets now buy airplanes instead. Private pilots think little of making a 1,000-mile round trip to a weekend resort.

Commercial aviation is a booming industry, and there is no letup on the horizon. Despite the boom, despite all those passenger-miles chalked up in recent years, an overwhelming percentage of the United States population has never even flown in an airplane. That's an untapped market if ever there was one.

And the military shows no signs of letting up either. Uncle Sam is committed to strength through airpower, and that means more airplanes and more men to make them go.

Rockets and space capsules will be proliferating, but not without pilots.

Everywhere you turn in the air business, you see a greater need for pilots.

Who will they be, these pilots of the day after tomorrow? What kind of education and training will it take to qualify? For a good idea, take a hard look at today's qualifications—and allow for plenty of added demands as the equipment grows even more sophisticated.

The private pilot needs only good general health (including good vision, but eyeglasses are common) and a willingness to learn. Instrument, commercial, and multiengine ratings require higher physical qualifications, including good reaction time and such things as good peripheral vision.

Commercial aviation looks for more—mainly pilots who will be around for a long time (mandatory retirement age is

60). Result: the young man gets the break. The risks have long since been reduced; airline pilots don't even pay extra premiums for life insurance these days. But the standards remain high.

The airlines need pilots with rather extensive experience. But first they look for a good educational background: two years or more of accredited college work or its equivalent, and preferably a bachelor's degree. If at all possible, some of the college work should be in some scientific field (although that's not absolutely necessary).

Trans World Airlines, which expects to hire 500 pilots in 1967, stands with the Government and with the other airlines in insisting on several requirements: a first-class FAA physical certificate, a commercial pilot's certificate, an instrument rating. TWA's "ideal applicant" is between 20 and 24 years old, in excellent physical condition, 5-feet-7 to 6-feet-4, with the necessary FAA certificates, a college degree, and what TWA Captain F. F. Rowe called "a high level of motivation."

"Obviously, we are making some deviations [now]," Captain Rowe says, "and we may be forced to continue to do so. . . .

"It is my belief, however, that the individual who meets our ideal requirements . . . will have an excellent opportunity."

Part of that opportunity, a part not stressed in this book, is to join TWA's growing international crew lists. TWA's international pilots are based in New York, with crew turnarounds in Paris, London, Frankfurt, Madrid, Rome, Tel Aviv, Cairo, Zurich, and Milan—as well as Los Angeles and Bombay, the furthermost ends of its route network.

International jet captains earn about 10 percent more than domestic jet captains, but there are a number of variables such as seniority, day flights versus night flights, over water versus over land, which change the pay for each man. International pilots make an average of four to five

151

transatlantic trips a month. They can earn well over $25,000 a year.

The military services have different requirements, but most of them want candidates with college backgrounds.

The Army insists that it will make a pilot out of a high school graduate with 20-20 vision, and good hearing, who passes the physical and mental tests. They'll train him and he can attain the rank of warrant officer (which falls between the highest noncommissioned rank and that of a second lieutenant). The total training period takes one year, and the candidate must enlist for a total of four years. The Army prefers no previous flying experience, but warns that its flying school is a rough one. Qualifications are high and the dropout rate is too.

The Navy wants men 19 to 25, with two years or sixty semester hours of college, 20-20 vision and no eye defects, good hearing, mentally qualified, to spend 18 months at Pensacola, Florida, as an aviation cadet. During the training they get $120 a month plus flight pay, which brings the total to about $325. They graduate as ensigns; after another year and a half they can be promoted to lieutenant junior grade. The Navy says that it occasionally accepts a few candidates for Naval Reserve Officers Training courses at colleges, with a view toward making pilots out of them. But the vacancies are infrequent, and most pilots do it the other way.

The Air Force, contrary to popular myth, doesn't train pilots at its Air Force Academy. It trains Air Force officers there. Those who want to become pilots later may be accepted in flight training courses elsewhere.

The Air Force also insists that all its pilots be commissioned officers. If the recruit has thirty credits or one year of college, and qualifies otherwise, the Air Force will accept him under its Airman Education and Commissioning Program. But there is no advance assurance of acceptance, and the Air Force won't give you the tests until after you enlist.

If a high school graduate enlists, he may apply for pilot training only after he completes one year of active duty. The Air Force will finance his college education if he is accepted.

After he has his degree, the Air Force candidate attends a three-month precommissioning school, and emerges as a second lieutenant. After that he faces about one year of flight school (and a promotion to first lieutenant). The length of training depends on the type of aircraft.

All the services stress that they squeeze their military college students through three years of college in two calendar years; there isn't much time off in that kind of a crash program.

The Marines want officer-pilots too. And to apply for the Marine Aviation Cadet Program you need two years of college or sixty semester hours. The Marine Corps also has a career incentive program: Marines over the rank of corporal can apply and be sent to an 18-month flying school.

A businessman-pilot can, of course, fly his own plane. But in order to fly an airplane *for pay*, he must have a commercial license, and he'll need an instrument rating as well. Today's business pilots fly everything from single-engine light planes to DC-3's and even jets. They fly on regular and irregular schedules, depending on the company. But they are well paid, with excellent fringe benefits in most cases.

The pilot of the future undoubtedly will need better training, and more of it. Technology is growing fast, and human beings are hard-pressed to keep up with it. Aviation is no exception.

But the pilot, the guy who flies, is far from obsolete.

Ed Richter is a veteran newspaperman and author who is employed as a staff writer for the Board of Christian Education of The United Presbyterian Church U.S.A. He has authored or coauthored six books.

Mr. Richter has had a thirteen-year newspaper career in which he worked as a reporter, feature writer, wire editor, suburban editor, and managing editor. He won a Pennsylvania state prize for feature writing in 1955.

He is an ordained Presbyterian elder, and is active in many segments of the United Presbyterian Church. He is also a lay preacher.

He is married to the former Esther Ruth Logsdon, and they have four children. The Richters make their home in Havertown, Pennsylvania.